Reflections

Irish language communities in action

ems should be returned on or before the last date
shown below. Items not already requested by other
borrowers may be renewed in person, in writing or by
telephone. To renew, please quote the number on the
barcode label. To renew online a PIN is required.
This can be requested at your local library.
Renew online @ www.dublincitypubliclibraries.ie
Fines charged for overdue items will include postage
incurred in recovery. Damage to or loss of items will
be charged to the borrower.

Leabharlanna Poiblí Chathair Bhaile Átha Cliath
Dublin City Public Libraries

Dublin City
Baile Átha Cliath

Terenure Branch Tel: 4907035

Date Due	Date Due	Date Due
20. DEC 07		

Contents

Foreword

Activism and reflection are interdependent. Each supports the other. Activism without reflection may go astray; the results of reflection are tested in the realm of action.

The reflections gathered together in this publication have already been presented to Irish speakers. I am pleased to offer them now to an English-speaking readership. The articles here collectively represent a measured reflection on the long tradition of cultural activism in Ireland, a tradition which has found expression in the work of Glór na nGael for more than forty years now. As the conceptualisation of Irish has developed over time, so too has the activist response. That response is taken up, described by the contributors in their own inimitable way and reflected upon in these pages in ways that provide a basis for the future.

Whether Irish speakers are conceived of as a single community or as a group of communities, it is clear that cultural and linguistic identity is not passed on through the generations untransformed. Each generation redefines itself, and I welcome each community that speaks to us in this book. I am grateful to the editor, Helen Ó Murchú, who generously accepted the invitation to take part in the project. I congratulate all participants on the presentation of their experiences and reflections, through which they enhance the life of Irish, and, through it, our common human inheritance.

Máire Ní Annracháin
Chairperson
Glór na nGael

The challenge facing the Irish language voluntary sector

Lorcán Mac Gabhann

I was twenty years of age when I got my first job in the Irish language movement with Conradh na Gaeilge as a timire (Irish language organizer). The job of the timire was to support and to further develop a national network of community-based voluntary committees which promoted the use of the Irish language in their own areas. Looking back on who I was then, I wonder how much help I actually managed to offer to those wonderful people in both rural and urban areas striving to promote Irish as a living language. Luckily I had a very sincere and encouraging boss in Seán Mac Mathúna, the general secretary of Conradh na Gaeilge, who understood how little experience I had in language planning and language development. Important as Seán's help was, it was almost secondary to the support I received from volunteers from all walks of life, the length and breadth of the country. And it was I who was employed to support them!

I remember one of the first instructions I received from Seán Mac Mathúna was to establish a branch of Conradh na Gaeilge in Dún Laoghaire. Very naively I assured him that it would be set up and operating by Christmas, i.e. within two months. Early the next day I set out on the 46A bus, all prepared to create a vibrant and modern local language movement. Two hours later, finding myself staring out over a grey Dublin bay, I realised that the amount I knew about language planning and local language initiatives could be written on the back of a postage stamp. As has happened again and again throughout my career in the Irish language movement, I was rescued from public humiliation by an unpaid language activist. A member of Conradh na Gaeilge, residing in Palmerstown at the time, made the trek over to Dún Laoghaire and chaired a public meeting that eventually saw the establishment of Craobh Dhún Laoghaire, Conradh na Gaeilge. Prior to the meeting I distributed leaflets to over 1,000 homes advertising a public meeting and outlining our plans to develop Irish language usage in the locality. As a consequence more than 100 people attended the public meeting in the Royal Marine Hotel. An enthusiastic voluntary committee was elected on the night and a plan of action was shortly agreed. Unfortunately, as is the case of many other voluntary Irish language committees, Craobh Dhún Laoghaire no longer exists. I do not see this non-existence in any way as a failure of those involved but as a failure of the state to support and encourage their efforts.

Has anything remained the same since 1986? Technology used in the mid-eighties has been redundant since the early nineties. A pint of the black stuff would have set you back a pound whereas today a small fortune is required to go out on the town. The road structure has improved from the narrow country roads we once knew to the standard maintained by other major international road networks. State funding of community voluntary endeavour is, however, another matter entirely. Sporting organisations both national and local, that once drew all their expertise from the local voluntary pool, are now being supported by millions of euro annually from central government. On the other hand, although some modest funding was available for national Irish language organisations, both state and voluntary, it was non-existent for local initiatives. This situation, unfortunately remains virtually the same today.

Mid-way through the last century, and right up until the early eighties, the towns throughout the country that did not operate an Irish language committee of some description were the exception rather than the rule. But as the Celtic Tiger began to take shape, the number of voluntary committees in existence, in all voluntary sectors, dramatically decreased over a very short space of time. (Hence the recent Irish Government's national initiative to attract people back to voluntary work.) Sporting organisations such as the Gaelic Athletic Association (GAA) and the Football Association of Ireland (FAI) did indeed suffer a decrease in the number of volunteer hours available to them during this time. However, the decrease in voluntary hours available to the Irish language community sector was, by comparison, catastrophic. Many of the reasons for lack of volunteers for Irish language community schemes are shared with other voluntary sectors. They include pressures created by employment, lack of recreation time for families, amount of time spent commuting to and from the work place. But for me, one reasons stands out above all others in the community language sector – short term aims are difficult to achieve. It can often take many years of arduous effort to accomplish any real and lasting linguistic impact in any given community.

The exception to this, in the Irish language voluntary sector, is the on-going establishment of all-Irish language pre-schools and schools at primary level. While a number of post-primary schools have been established in recent years, any significant development of this second level sector is being frustrated by the

Department of Education and Science which is currently refusing to financially support the development of new all-Irish independent post-primary schools on an equal basis to newly established schools under the auspices of the VEC (Vocational Education Committees).

When a group of parents meets to set-up a gaelscoil (primary school) the aim is mainly singular and short term, e.g., to establish a gaelscoil in an area in a given period of time. Once the founding committee attains temporary official recognition for the new school, funding mechanisms are released to support its establishment, although many in the gaelscoileanna movement would argue that this financial support is inadequate. For a person endeavouring to promote the language in all facets of community life, the establishment of a gaelscoil is of course only one constituent part of that community. As someone who was involved in the establishment of a gaelscoil in the mid-nineties I am only too aware of the difficulties involved in setting up a new school. But while the founding committee of Gaelscoil Thaobh na Coille faced major obstacles and challenges, they were surmountable, with difficulty, within an agreed Department of Education and Science framework. When a school founding committee fulfils a number of agreed criteria with the Department, it is then granted temporary recognition.

No such state recognition, temporary or otherwise, exists for the voluntary local Irish language community group. In fact there is absolutely no adequate long-term support available for the local Irish language committee from any state source. I refer to state funding for the establishment of a gaelscoil only to point up, by comparison, the lack of support for local Irish language committees. I admire and applaud the constant struggles faced by both newly founded and long-established gaelscoileanna. They have survived often in spite of the best efforts of others, locally and nationally, to frustrate them.

The local language enthusiast or activist belongs to a different breed of volunteer – those that recognise that the restoration of the Irish language needs a broader basis than that of solely Irish-medium education. They recognise that the promotion of the Irish language as a living community language needs long-term strategic planning in partnership with a broad range of other community groups. Many language activists operate within a committee structure and the majority of those committees are part of the Glór na nGael network. Glór na Gael is a national, and since 2005 an international, network of local committees whose aim is to promote the language locally and nationally. At its core is a competition that rewards and recognises the annual endeavours of the participating committees. Being part of the Glór na nGael

3

national network means that a committee is promoting the language on a partnership basis with other local community groups, such as the Chamber of Commerce, local sporting organisations such as the GAA, local schools, parish committees, Tidy Town Committees, Youth Organisations etc. Consequently, for a local group or committee to progress in this national competition they must be involved in

- youth work e.g. after-school clubs and youth clubs
- educational schemes, e.g. the provision of all-Irish education at all levels including, if possible, third level (e.g. an Irish language diploma is offered by several universities), the promotion of Irish in main-stream English schools, provision of adult education at all stages of levels of linguistic capacity
- encouraging and promoting the use of Irish in the home
- promotion of Irish in local business and local government agencies
- provision of regular social activities on a continuous basis for learners and fluent speakers alike
- raising public awareness of the Irish language amongst the community
- major events such as Seachtain na Gaeilge (Irish language Week) so that the entire community may celebrate the Irish language as part of its national identity.

Experienced Development Officers employed by Glór na nGael are available to the committees on year-round basis for support and advice. But none of the above aims, short term or long term, can be achieved within the short or even medium term. It may take a generation or two before any lasting linguistic impact on a community can be achieved. Enormous effort and goodwill from many, across a vast spectrum of community groups, is required if the objective of the committee is to increase dramatically the number of Irish language speakers using the language on a daily basis. While this single objective may appear straightforward, to achieve its fulfilment without local full-time and long-term assistance is simply impossible.

Why then, do we expect a small group of committed, but already overstressed Celtic Tiger individuals, to achieve the impossible within a voluntary structure? Is it reasonable to demand from volunteers that they become the Irish language conscience of the nation? How can one committee, with limited resources and finance, change the linguistic character of a community and even a nation? In what other sphere of Irish life has the state demanded of its people that they change the behaviour of the nation?

To the best of my knowledge, up until the end of the nineties, there were no more than half a dozen people employed specifically on a full-time basis in any locality outside the Gaeltacht to promote the Irish language on a community wide basis. In 2006 with the welcome, but somewhat limited, support of the cross-border language agency, Foras na Gaeilge, there are full-time Irish language community development officers active locally, outside of the Gaeltacht, in Clondalkin, Ennis, Loughrea, Galway City, Castlebar, Letterkenny, Derry, Strabane, Sion Mills, Downpaulck, Belfast, and Maghorafelt. The impact these full-time development officers have had on the numbers of people using Irish in their locality has been extremely positive. The time has come for us to recognise that the future of the Irish language as a living community language cannot continue to depend on the sacrifices of voluntary individuals alone. It is not my intention to devalue the incredible work carried out by the voluntary language sector, as without their continuing efforts Irish would not be as vibrant as it is today throughout the island of Ireland. The professional skills that exist in the voluntary committee, that are provided free of charge, are a central part of language planning and of any National Irish Language Plan that may evolve over the coming years. But we can no longer depend solely on their endeavours. It is wrong to place the future of Irish in the community on the already overburdened shoulders of a few.

It is time for central Government to invest locally in Irish language schemes and that must be done as a matter of urgency. Compared to investment in sports organisations throughout the country Irish language schemes are lagging so far behind as not to even register. Excluding Gaeltacht areas, less than €1.5 million was spent on Irish language community schemes in the 32 counties of Ireland last year (2005). In one calendar year The Department of Sport and Tourism grant-aided in excess of that figure, €1.6 million, to local sports clubs in County Kildare alone! It is accepted that sport and fitness are issues of national importance. But compared to the €1.5 million grant aid to local community language schemes nationally, local sporting schemes received €1.2 million in County Clare, €1 million in County Cavan, €7.8 million in County Cork, €1.6 million in County Donegal, €5.3 million in Dublin and so on, county by county. This current low level of investment in language is so inequitable as to be a national disgrace. Investment in language activity should be increased substantially and urgently.

Consider a modern urban area in twenty-first century Ireland with a population of approximately five thousand people. It will most likely have the following: primary and post-primary schools, shops, pubs, sports clubs, a drama group, a youth club, a senior citizen club, a parish council, a chamber of commerce, local government offices, business outlets, and so on. It is unrealistic to expect a small voluntary committee, without the support of a full-time development office, to develop and co-ordinate an Irish language action plan that would influence the linguistic character of all of those groups. I challenge the national government to suggest that we can continue to restore the language as a community language without new community investment schemes. Appropriate schemes would allow existing community groups to develop and to implement language plans in towns such as Sligo, Ballycastle, Newry, Dundalk, Enniscorthy, Waterford, Mallow, Listowel, Ballinasloe, Claremorris, Cavan, Mullingar, Portlaoise, Thurles, Longford, Clones, Limerick, Birr and Kildare. What is required without delay is the establishment of a national Irish language community employment fund solely for groups wishing to promote the Irish language on a community basis. The Irish language is not confined to the Republic, and therefore the national Irish language community employment fund should be administered on a cross-border basis by a newly formed agency dedicated solely to the funding of community groups, north and south.

At this stage, getting agreement for the new fund takes priority over how it would eventually be distributed, although it could be strongly argued that Foras na Gaeilge would be in a position, as a cross-border body, to distribute any newly released community employment funds. If this were the case, the newly created fund would have to be ring-fenced for community employment schemes only.

I call on all those involved in the promotion of the Irish language throughout the island of Ireland, and those with the necessary political influence, to enter into discussions together with the aim of establishing a national Irish language community employment fund as a matter of urgency. The individual stories recounted in this publication are vibrant proof of the need for such a crucial and courageous step forward in the maintenance of the Irish language.

Developments in Paróiste an Chnoic

Peadar Mac an Iomaire

Background and history

When the Irish Free State was established, poverty and emigration were causing great hardship for the people of Cois Fharraige and indeed to people across the country. As the state began implementing the aims of the language movement visitors began arriving in Cois Fharraige to improve their Irish. Among them were some of the founders of the state as well as civil servants. Academics were also looking to Cois Fharraige, in particular those who needed to improve their qualifications and their ability in Irish. Ardscoil Mhichíl Bhreathnaigh was established in Cois Fharraige in the thirties to assist students in University College, Galway and in other institutions throughout Ireland to get to know each other and to improve their Irish. University College Galway saw the enactment of the 1929 Act and as a result courses through the medium of Irish were offered to students, as well as scholarships to attend those courses. Some of the newly appointed lecturers, such as Liam Ó Buachalla and an tAthair Eric Mac Fhinn, had close ties with the people of Cois Fharraige. In the 1930s the Trade Union movement in Dublin also set up a scheme to enable the children of union members to learn Irish by attending a month long Irish language course in Cois Fharraige. These courses remained available every July and August right up to the mid sixties, when Coláiste Lurgan was established as an Irish College. As far as the people of Cois Fharraige were concerned, their role was to provide accommodation for the learners and answer their questions regarding Irish. It is unclear if any major efforts were made to tackle the economic and social problems of the people apart from that.

The establishment of Roinn na Gaeltachta in 1956 was one of the greatest actions to assist social development in Cois Fharraige and in many other Gaeltacht areas. By the end of the 1960s very few thatched cottages in bad repair remained inhabited. This change was due to a generous Roinn na Gaeltachta grant which assisted people in building houses on their own holdings. In the sixties Roinn na Gaeltachta also initiated a number of schemes which assisted agri-development and the refurbishment of houses for tourism. It also provided a school travel grant which allowed students from Cois Fharraige to travel from their own areas

7

to Galway to receive their post-primary education up to Leaving Certificate level, something which had not been available to boys in Cois Fharraige at the time. Those scholars then continued to University College Galway, returning home every evening. This ensured that young men were able to take part in the football club or in development groups in the area and rather than spending their free time with college societies they were working in a practical way for the development of their own community.

In 1966 Cumann Forbartha Chois Fharraige (Development Association) was established and one of its first tasks was to enter the Glór na nGael competition. We knew very little about Glór na nGael at the time except that it was organising a competition and that it would give us a chance to compete with other communities and, as a result, promote Cois Fharraige. The late Pól Ó Foighil moved west from An Spidéal in 1966 and established Coláiste Lurgan with pre-fabricated classrooms in Gleann an Chnoic.

It was difficult, however, to make any progress with the state organisations because development activity was closely tied to party politics. It was this which inspired the birth of the Gaeltacht Civil Rights movement in 1969. At the beginning of the 1970s Comharchumann Chois Fharraige (Co-operative) was established and, apart from running the Coláistí Gaeilge, the Comharchumann set up a group water scheme for Cois Fharraige. Galway County Council did not have the resources to provide public water supplies for the area. The group scheme assisted housekeepers in providing accommodation to more students and visitors in the area and also as a central plank in attracting industry to the Gaeltacht.

An Comharchumann also set up Cló Chois Fharraige (Print) to meet the shortage of text books in Gaeltacht schools and Clódóirí Lurgan was then founded to print the books and to carry out other printing works. This provided skilled employment in the area. Comharchumann Chois Fharraige continued from 1971 until the end of 1983. It was due to a shortage of state support that An Comharchumann ceased trading. Comharchumann Shailearna was founded to attend to services which no other organisation was dealing with at the time: a water service from An Spidéal to Ros a' Mhíl; Bog Development Services and infrastructural services. At the beginning of the 1970s Comhchoiste Ghaeltacht Chonamara was set up so that every parish in the Gaeltacht would have a community council in preparation for an Údarás Gaeltachta (Gaeltacht

Authority). The leadership for this movement grew out of Cumann Forbartha Chois Fharraige.

Comharchumann Shailearna which was founded in February 1984 is still working at full steam and is now focusing more of its attention on language promotion and maintenance. Among its language activities is the development of pre-school services and, arising from that, a strategy has been developed to establish a language based family support centre with the support of the Department of Justice, Equality and Law Reform in co-operation with the Department of Community, Rural and Gaeltacht Affairs.

An Comharchumann is also promoting university education through Irish and with the renovation of Seanscoil Shailearna a modern theatre has been provided for different community activities throughout the year.

From the mid-sixties until the end of the last century the community of An Cnoc was in a state of evolution generated by the empowerment of the community. They took on board suggestions from other Irish language groups, such as the pre-school activities, just as Údarás na Gaeltachta was to do later - although it took them twenty years to come to understand that there was little use in using a pre-school scheme for Irish speakers from outside the Gaeltacht to assist people from within the Gaeltacht.

What was happening was that pre-schools were helping to teach Irish to children from the Gaeltacht whose parents were not using Irish as the language of the home and that children whose first language was Irish were turning to English because of the language structure in the naíonraí (pre-schools); or indeed that parents were deciding that they were not going to send their children to the naíonra because the naíonra was there to teach Irish to children and that the naíonraí were not there to assist the development of the child through Irish language maintenance. This led the community to set up their own pre-school system and to share their experience with Údarás na Gaeltachta and any other interested parties. It was decided to develop two types of pre-school in An Cnoc to assist in improving language usage among the children – one for the development of children whose first language was Irish and the other to assist children from English-speaking backgrounds to acquire Irish.

The current situation

The type of work which I have mentioned was not confined to Cois Fharraige. It was also happening in other parishes, thanks to grants from the Department of the Gaeltacht to comharchumainn and other schemes which provide support to community based efforts.

It has been community based initiatives which have kept the language alive and were it not for them the language would be in a much worse state in the Gaeltacht today; which shows that Máirtín Ó Cadhain was correct when he said that Irish was in danger in the fifties and sixties, at a time when neither the state nor the language movement agreed with him. Leadership was being given by people who had cut their teeth in the Community Development groups in the Gaeltacht not only within the community but also in organisations outside the community who were helping to strengthen the community. Among these were: Eagras na gComharchumann Gaeltachta, Comhchoiste na gColáistí Samhraidh (summer colleges) and national organisations such as Comhchoiste Ghaeltacht Chonamara and ad hoc groups set up from time to time to achieve Raidió na Gaeltachta, Teilifís na Gaeilge and other community enhancing resources. Among the vanguard were people such as Éamon Ó Cuív, Pádraig Ó hAoláin, Pádraig Mac Donnacha, Máire Mhic Niallais, Pádraig Feirtéir, An tAthair Mícheál Ó Flannabhra, An Monsignor Pádraig Ó Fiannachta and many more. The movement made advances because it was dealing with matters which were vital to the people. Community development projects were closely related to Irish language maintenance and in that way the Irish language community movements received support from the community.

It was as a result of community demand that Raidió na Gaeltachta and later TG4 were set up. It was no small feat to train people for media employment and it was not easy for Údarás na Gaeltachta to give the support which they gave at the time, since it was felt that they were giving money to RTÉ (Raidió Teilifís Éireann) for training Gaeltacht people in the Gaeltacht for the Irish language media. In the fifties and sixties people like Proinsias Mac Aonghusa, Breandán Ó hEithir, Máirtín Ó Conghaile, Pádraig Ó Gaora, Proinsias Ó Conluain and Mícheál Ó Cuinneagáin had been providing service for the Gaeltacht people in the media through Irish. While they had a good audience for what they had to say, they were still 'lodgers' within the English speaking community. When Raidió na Gaeltachta and TG4 arrived, people from the community lived within the community and apart from giving a service through the media they were also providing a service to Gaeltacht communities, taking part in Irish language community activities which improved their language ability while they continued working in the media.

Gaeltacht primary and secondary education is under pressure at present. While the Leaving Certificate is provided for in every post-primary Gaeltacht school now, there is a need for a Gaeltacht VEC (Vocational Education Committee) to attend to teaching through Irish in Gaeltacht schools by those with a high proficiency in Irish. The language is undoubtedly under pressure among the Gaeltacht youth. Entertainment is geared towards English; the Gaeltacht is open to thousands of young people who arrive every summer to learn Irish but there are also many people settled in the Gaeltacht whose home language is not Irish and who in any case are not proficient enough to make Irish the language of their homes. It must be said that there are generous community development state grants available at present. If it were not for the work which Cumann Peile Mhícheál Breathnach is carrying out among the youth to maintain the language, the use of Irish would be much poorer in Cois Fharraige today.

The pre-schools and crèches are evolving into family support centres in the parish of An Cnoc. Just as the Credit Union adds to the local economy and the tradition of saving in the area, so too will the Family Support Centres advise parents on the best ways of carrying the language forward from one generation to the next. The Planning Act (2000) is being implemented by the local authority at present and that act will provide a certain amount of protection to the resources of the Gaeltacht to ensure that young Gaeltacht people are not left unable to purchase housing sites.

A way has been found in Cois Fharraige to demonstrate community respect for our community heritage through the construction of 36 houses for the elderly and 9 houses for the unwell. A health centre has been built beside Tearmann Éanna which will serve the needs of the western part of Paróiste an Chnoic.

An Cnoc community believe that they have a valuable contribution to make through Irish language community development which will benefit Irish language communities working under the aegis of Glór na nGael. It is vital that the work of the Irish language be tied in to other work such as economic and social development so that the interest which ordinary people have in the community will be enhanced.

With the support which is available from the Department of Community, Rural and Gaeltacht Affairs and other organisations such as Meitheal Forbartha na Gaeltachta and Cumas Teo., people can now do things for their community that were not possible twenty, thirty or forty years ago. In the same way the Community Employment Schemes administered by Údarás na Gaeltachta for FÁS (Foras Áiseanna Saothair, the Training and Employment Authority) have greatly advanced community and language works in the Gaeltacht. The new Údarás na Gaeltachta strategy being steered by its CEO, Pádraig Ó hAoláin, offers a sign of hope to the people of Cois Fharraige. It is also a hopeful sign that Pádraig who is a former manager of a Comharchumann is now Head of Údarás na Gaeltachta – an organisation which in its early days was reluctant to give the necessary support to either comharchumainn or community based organisations since it did not envisage helping these organs of society as part of its role.

Future challenges and opportunities

If one were to ask those who have spent years involved with community development in Cois Fharraige what progress could be made with the work of Glór na nGael among the Irish speaking community, the answer would be simple. The language movement must work towards reducing the flow of Irish speakers from the Gaeltacht. Although young people can gain experience outside of their own areas, an important step would be to ensure more and more services for young people in their own communities. Young people could gain experience outside of their own rural areas by visiting other rural communities where third level centres are established such as Sabhal Mór Ostaig in the Isle of Skye, Coláiste an Chaisil on the Isle of Lewis, or Ollscoil na nGleann in Wales. Education and training must rejuvenate the community by attracting both Gaeltacht and Irish speaking youth to the Gaeltacht community and thus make Irish 'cool' among Gaeltacht youth.

It is also important that the people become more independent and that sport, entertainment, education and training build capacity so that we become more developed as a community than rural or urban people have been until now. Credit must be given to the leadership which the Minister for Community, Rural and Gaeltacht Affairs, Éamon Ó Cuív, T.D., has given in creating the infrastructure for protecting the language community of the Gaeltacht through community structures. It is important that the language be recognised by the Gaeltacht community as an integral part of Gaeltacht infrastructure. The community of An

Cnoc has proposed that the Department of Community, Rural and Gaeltacht Affairs should make state assistance available for bottom-up language planning in the Gaeltacht. That assistance has been made available to An Cnoc and several other Gaeltacht areas. What is very interesting about the scheme is that it is succeeding in persuading the community itself that bottom-up language planning is both important and beneficial for its survival.

This should change the practice which has been in place since the nineteen fifties, when Departmental officers would carry out Irish language inspections of Gaeltacht families and their children. That practice did not help create an attitude of language conservation among those who spoke the language. They felt that the state was imposing unwanted inspections on them. Through the new approach the community managed to propose a scheme which allowed the state to give ownership to the community of language planning at community level, with the result that the community had more respect for the language as a resource which they were now partners in protecting.

There is now a widely held belief in Cois Fharraige that Irish language education and training is the key for recognising Irish as a resource for language centred and knowledge-based employment and as a means of promoting the community. That was demonstrated very clearly when the President of NUI (National University of Ireland) Galway awarded degrees to two heroes of Cois Fharraige, Johnny Chóil Mhaidhc Ó Coisdealbha and Joe Steve Ó Neachtain. On that occasion the President emphasised this and explained that it is a strategic aim of NUI Galway to bring university education to the community and he congratulated the Cois Fharraige community for all their efforts, in conjunction with the university, to bring Irish language university education to the community. Údarás na Gaeltachta and the Department of Community, Rural and Gaeltacht Affairs should be viewed as tools to assist government departments and other state bodies in ensuring that Irish speakers can conduct their business with the state through Irish without difficulty or hindrance. Just as Údarás na Gaeltachta assisted FÁS to administer the Social Employment Schemes through Irish in Gaeltacht communities, An tÚdarás and the Department are also capable of giving the same assistance in implementing the Official Languages Act in the Gaeltacht and among Irish speakers throughout the country. Such practice will create employment for Irish speakers.

It is essential that Irish-speaking communities in the Gaeltacht and elsewhere share a vision built on imagination and a philosophy that will create community development with an Irish language link. It is an opportunity for Glór na nGael to act as a leader for those Irish-language communities, a leader which will enable them to forget the tragic years of language decay in the post-famine era and the reduction of the number of native Irish speakers in the Gaeltacht since the foundation of the state to the present day.

Through education and training we now have the key to inform us as to what has occurred; to prepare ourselves for the present; and to look to the future with hope. Our challenge is to transmit the language from one generation to the next. The social structure is changing and this is why the Language Support Centres are so important: with both parents increasingly working from eight to six daily the children need to be cared for by fluent Irish speakers so that by the time they reach primary school age they will have fluent Irish. It is vital that third level institutions have centres in the Gaeltacht to train primary and post-primary school teachers for Gaeltacht and all-Irish schools, and for other schools too where practicable. It is also important that Irish teachers with a B.A. or B. Ed. can spend a year in an Irish speaking community to ensure that not only have they acquired good Irish but that issues such as language behaviour, maintenance and planning are an integral part of their degree. One downside of the present educational system is that young teachers can go out teaching with barely 40% in Irish at degree level. If that teacher – or his or her pupils - are unfortunate enough to be employed in an area where there are no opportunities to practice the language the chances are that he/she will have lost spoken language ability within five to seven years. That teacher will remain employed by the state, however, teaching Irish for the next forty years.

This practice must be stopped and one way of ending it is to give young graduates a year in the Gaeltacht to ensure that graduates in Irish have the same advantages as graduates of other European languages, who have the benefit of the European Union Erasmus programme.

Glór na nGael groups throughout the country are invited to make use of the same type of community developments which have taken place in Cois Fharraige during the past forty years, and to work with us to ensure that all the Irish speaking communities of this island will be progressing together during the next forty years to ensure that the language is safely delivered from one generation to the next. Irish does not belong solely to us, nor to any single generation. All we can do is use it and ensure that we pass it on to the next generation, so that they have the right to weave their own piece of the tapestry which, like us, they have inherited.

The future of Irish: integrated language planning

Seosamh Mac Donncha
(then) CEO, Foras na Gaeilge

Background

For some years now since my appointment as CEO (Chief Executive Officer) of Foras na Gaeilge I have been making reference to the need for integrated Irish language planning. I am certain that you have all heard me refer to the metaphorical train journey which is in store for all of us who work in the language sector. I have often said that there will not be many more trains leaving the platform and that we therefore need to get as many passengers on board as possible.

The language sector has taken many twists and turns since the journey started but overall I can say that I am more hopeful now than I have been for a long while due to different decisions which the sector has arrived at and taken. Of course all of us in the Irish language sector know that there are many challenges before us still.

Among those landmark steps taken would be the Report of the Commission on the Gaeltacht in 2002; the enactment of the Official Languages Act 2003; and the appointment of the Language Commissioner, Seán ó Curraoin, in 2004. Of course another great morale boost was the success of the Stádas campaign which succeeded in winning both official and working status for Irish in the European Union in June 2005 when the other countries of the EU conceded to the Irish Government's petition for this. Above all else the Stádas campaign showed how the question of Irish could be brought to the centre stage through partnership and strategic action.

Reflections

Overview

In the context of all these events I want to give an overview here of the work which Foras na Gaeilge is doing in language planning as a preparation for the journey ahead.

This work springs primarily from two sources:

> A review of the Strategic Plan which was prepared internally for the Foras itself;
> the proposals of the Coimisiún na Gaeltachta (Gaeltacht Commission) report, and in particular proposals 7,16 and 17.

(i) To begin I want to refer to the honest review which the first Board of the Foras carried out of their performance for the period ending in 2002. Although it was accepted that the Strategic Plan was suitable in terms of the Foras's own internal administrative structures and that Status, Acquisition and Usage were appropriate key challenges for the organisation and the language sector, it was noted that a broader and deeper approach was needed to meet the needs of the whole sector.

(ii) With regard to the proposals of Tuarascáil Choimisiún na Gaeltachta, the emphasis which was placed on the need for a National Plan for the Irish language (Proposal 7) was noted. So also was the need to develop a Language Planning System using the best available international practices (Proposal 16) and the need to establish an Executive Structure for Language Planning (Proposal 17).

I have often mentioned the importance of true partnerships as the approach which would give leadership to the sector, and since the Foras is an All-Ireland Structure, the Board of the Foras decided to prepare for the language planning process.

Tuarascáil Choimisiún na Gaeltachta (Paragraph 5.7: A Language Planning System and Implementation Structure) recognised that the major absence of language planning was the greatest weakness demonstrated by the Commission's work. When the Irish situation was placed in the context of other countries' experience it was obvious that our understanding of such planning was falling behind.

In a critique given by Professor Colin Williams from Wales of language planning in Ireland during a language conference in Helsinki some years ago, he referred to the lack of co-ordination and integrated planning in the history of language planning for Irish.

It is encouraging that this weakness has been recognised by Minister Éamon Ó Cuív, T.D. and that the new CEO of Údarás na Gaeltachta, Pádraig Ó hAoláin, agrees with him. One can see this particularly in the new emphasis on language-based developments, projects and initiatives. As I mentioned earlier we all recognise the advantages and benefits which came from the strategic partnerships which secured official and working language status for Irish in the EU. From our regular contacts with voluntary Irish language organisations, it is clear that a central, integrated language planning strategy would be welcome.

While we were hopeful that the discussion document would have been completed by 2005 we were engrossed in other pressing concerns for the past year and only recently have we returned to the business of integrated planning. It is worth repeating, therefore, the aims which will steer the planning process:
>To prepare an agreed comprehensive, integrated and inspiring vision.
>To clarify the role of each partner including the role of the Foras and the funding departments.
>To secure the best use of available resources – both human and financial.
>To give a voice to the community and to organisations.
>To give ownership to every partner and organisation in the progress.
>To create a continuous forum for debate.

The intention is that the results of the process would be the basis of a strategic action plan for the Irish language sector and that this would lay down guidelines for future funding and investment.

To start the process Foras na Gaeilge will make available a discussion document to the relevant partners, including:
>Funding Departments both North and South.
>State education departments and organisations both North and South.
>The Finance Departments both North and South.
>Údarás na Gaeltachta.
>The voluntary and educational organisations.
>As many groups and organisations as possible all across the island.

The community – this will be achieved through a series of nationwide public meetings.
The media.

In this consultation process individuals, groups and organisations, and the state itself will be given an opportunity to present their views, priorities, weaknesses and strengths. To ensure public ownership of the process every party will be given an input and also an input into the implementation of the plan which will arise from it.

This process will help the Foras:

To clarify priorities for ourselves as an organisation in the context of the Irish language sector.
To agree priorities with the relevant partners.
To see the bigger picture.
To influence the finance departments, north and south.
To influence the educations systems, north and south.
To make funding decisions in an open way in keeping with agreed priorities.
To agree the role and the work of the organisations.
To agree realistic targets for all events with the organisations.
To agree an evaluation and review procedure.
To recognise and encourage good practice in the Irish language sector.
To encourage good relations between the relevant partners.
To develop lines of communication between the relevant partners.

Frame of reference for the planning process

This approach, and the layout of the discussion paper will be based on the following integrated model for Language Planning.

Integrated model for Language Planning

This model is based on an understanding that there are two types of activities involved in creating and implementing a language strategy, i.e.

(a)   Primary strategic activities which have the target of directly impacting on the state of the language

and

(b)   Support activities which aim to support the primary strategic activities and to improve their performance.

(a) Primary Strategic Activities

The primary strategic activities mean activities which have the aim of affecting the following:

Community views and opinions on the language.

Acquiring and improving the language within the community.

Level of language usage within the community.

Sustainability and viability of the language community in economic, social, cultural, language and other terms.

Intergenerational transmission from one generation to the next through the family and other means.

(b) Support activities

Support activities mean:

Administering the language planning process effectively.

Managing and developing the human resources of the language planning process.

Administration of the organisational structure which is needed for the language planning process and ensuring that it is working effectively.

Carrying out research which provides facts and information to guide the language planning process.

Corpus Planning – development and distribution of a standard grammar and terminology and the supply of language tools such as dictionaries, and specialist dictionaries etc.

Convergent planning to ensure that other organisations, which are not central to the language planning process, but which have or could have an influence on activities in the target language, are working in tandem with the aims of the language planning process.

That everyone understands the huge importance of communication within the organisation, the sector and communication with the wider community.

Of course actions in one area of language rarely impact on one of the aforementioned areas without impacting on others.

For example, if one group organises a series of Irish classes their primary aim is usually to improve language ability. But of course this activity then affects the views of the participants concerning the language and indeed may lead to increased use of the language as well.

Language projects, therefore, will often have primary and secondary aims. For the sake of the language planning process, however, it is important that there is clarity about the primary objective of every scheme and project and that the efficiency and value of each scheme is assessed primarily according to its primary objective. It is important, however, that the identifiable secondary objectives are also recognised and that the best possible benefits are obtained from the opportunities which the schemes and projects make available to us.

Key characteristics and aims
The key characteristics of the proposed planning process are as follows:
> Openness
> Comprehensiveness
> Participation
> Partnership

The aim of the language planning process which the discussion document will propose will be as follows:
> To recognise the primary objectives which we should have for Irish in each area of activity.
> To agree the activities and the projects which are needed to achieve these.
> To clarify the roles of the relevant partners with regard to these actions and projects and to agree the integrated structures of communication, funding and assessment.

Finally, what we want to do here is to create a vision for the future of the Irish language for the next twenty years or so, and to begin realising that vision, in partnership together, as soon as possible.

Gaeltacht Uíbh Ráthaigh

Seán Mac an tSíthigh, Caitlín Bhreathnach

Background and history

An account of the present state of affairs in relation to the Irish language in the Gaeltacht of Uíbh Ráthaigh is not complete without looking back at the history of the language in the area over the last 100 years. The circumstances which affected the Gaeltacht community in the south west of south Kerry must also be taken into account. Those circumstances have created the Gaeltacht that we know today.

Today, Gaeltacht Uíbh Ráthach, if assessed by the latest figures from the Irish Speaking Scheme, is viewed as one of the weaker Gaeltachtaí in the country. That said, another statistic is to be found in the 1851 census. At that time, 90% of the population of Uíbh Ráthaigh were Irish speakers. The whole peninsula is included in that census instead of the marginal Gaeltacht areas that we have today. It is also worth mentioning that in the same census 54% of the population of Corca Dhuibhne were Irish speakers. Today Corca Dhuibhne Gaeltacht is viewed as one of the strongest Gaeltacht areas in Munster. Even in 1926, an average 73% of the people of Uíbh Ráthaigh were Irish speakers. So what happened in the case of Uíbh Ráthach? What were the circumstances that added to the decline of Irish in this particular area more than in any other area?

Without a doubt, Uíbh Ráthach had the same difficulties that other Gaeltacht areas had, i.e. remoteness, poor land, a poor economic situation, lack of employment, emigration etc. Author Bríd Ní Mhóráin, however, has shown that Uíbh Ráthach is different in that the decline of Irish happened very quickly in an area which had been a strong Gaeltacht area, as recounted in her book entitled 'Thiar sa Mhainistir atá an Ghaolainn Bhreá'.

One need only look at the wealth of folklore which was collected from the older generation in the 1940s and 1950s, a collection which is equal in richness to any other folklore collection from any other Gaeltacht, to understand how vibrant a Gaeltacht Uíbh Ráthach was. And that was only 60 or so years ago. The material collected was from people who spoke native Irish and spoke only Irish.

The majority of local people in Uíbh Ráthach nowadays feel that the state unfairly treated their Gaeltacht area. When the Gaeltacht boundaries were redrawn in 1956 Uíbh Ráthach Gaeltacht was dealt a heavy blow. Uíbh Ráthach emerged as a patchwork-like, ragged, rural, remote area, without any real town centre, without any Irish medium post-primary education. The resultant Gaeltacht was left as an unnatural social and linguistic entity.

Without a doubt, it must be admitted that the local community itself was partly to blame that the language declined so much but definitely the same official help that was given to other Gaeltacht areas was not given to Uíbh Ráthach.

The way in which Uíbh Ráthach was dealt with from the 1950s onwards cannot be blamed on the local community. The people of that time could not see the advantages of Irish. Although the area is beautiful and has been visited by many tourists, the area did not succeed in attracting the Irish scholars and students (apart from one or two) which other Gaeltachtaí attracted. From the 1960s onwards a remarkable industry, which was language based, developed in many Gaeltachtaí. This growth created high standard jobs in Irish – especially in community development and in the media. Unfortunately, this did not happen in Uíbh Ráthach. The first language based job was not created in Uíbh Ráthach until 1999.

It was then of little surprise that the people of Uíbh Ráthach were without energy and were depressed until that point. Through the lack of state support and lack of state investment Uíbh Ráthach was left marginalised and voiceless to act on its own behalf – whether for good or bad. Why should the people stay loyal to the Irish language? Therefore, the small groups within the community which took it upon themselves to act against all the opposing forces deserve great praise. They remained loyal to their heritage and they tried in every way to put themselves forward as a Gaeltacht people.

They asserted themselves to achieve the rights that they deserved as a Gaeltacht. It would have been expected in some quarters that Uíbh Ráthach Gaeltacht would run out of steam but that is not how matters developed. The community sought and found leadership amongst people who were active largely in community development and in educational matters.

In 1992 a new cultural community festival was set up. This Éigse na Brídeoige proved an important catalyst which rekindled the respect of the community again for the Irish language in Uíbh Ráthach. For the first time in a long while people had the opportunity to speak Irish socially through an event which was provided by the community for the community. Links were created with other Gaeltacht areas throughout Ireland via the Éigse. Soon a new respect for Irish was felt locally which went hand in hand with the comprehension and respect which were always there for the culture in the region.

Comhchoiste Ghaeltachtaí Chiarraí Theas was set up towards the end of the 1990s. It could be said that this committee grew from the committee of Éigse na Brídeoige. From the first day Comhchoiste Ghaeltachtaí Chiarraí Theas was representative of the whole Gaeltacht community. After losing a lot of people to emigration in the 1980s the community was low in itself, just as many other areas around Ireland were.

Community committees were becoming active again locally but they needed basic support to undertake the work which was essential to improve the physical infrastructure in Uíbh Ráthach. Also, at this time, it was clear that this was the last opportunity for this particular community to pass on the local dialect and the rich heritage and tradition of the area to the future generations. It was a decisive time indeed.

The current situation

The members of the Comhchoiste and the community committees behind them understood that in light of the generally accepted vision there was a limit to what could be achieved in terms of voluntary work. As already mentioned, the amount of support from the state for 50 years was not in any way remarkable. Some of the blame lay with the community which had not demanded such support. But this is easy to understand in the context of the lack of hope which was prevalent in the area especially from the 1950s onwards.

Reflections

In 1998 an application was sent to Údarás na Gaeltachta seeking funding to employ a Community Facilitator. This person would help the community committees to develop their physical and social plans and also to support the promotion of Irish in the area. The funding was allocated at the end of 1998 and from then on there has been good communication between the Comhchoiste and Údarás na Gaeltachta which is evident locally now.

Within two years, the Comhchoiste prepared a Heritage and Language Plan. The government agencies which had responsibility for the Irish language were on board. A Heritage Officer was appointed by the end of 2001 with support from Roinn na Gaeltachta. Soon after that a language learning support programme for Irish was set up for children and adults which was aided by Foras na Gaeilge and Kerry Education Service.

But the challenges were only beginning to come to the fore.

The work was well founded by the end of 2002, but it was obvious to all that medium term planning was essential to develop what was already achieved in the two major items of work underway. Most of 2003 was spent on a comprehensive planning process with the support of Údarás na Gaeltachta. During that year public community meetings were held to clarify the opinions and needs of the local people in relation to Irish and public affairs generally. A series of meetings were organised with those local, regional and national state bodies which would be able to aid the Gaeltacht community meet their recognised needs.

Gradually, a comprehensive plan was devised and continuous open communication routes in relation to feedback with the major funding bodies were set in place. During Éigse na Brídeoige on the 31 January 2004 Minister Éamon Ó Cuív, TD launched the Development Plan for Irish and the Irish Community of Uíbh Ráthach 2004 -2006.

Looking back now with the advantage of time, perhaps that plan was too co-ordinated and too comprehensive when considered in the context in which community organisations like Comhchoiste function.

Because an integrated approach was set out in the plan, which was continually discussed in detail with the various partners during the process, the Comhchoiste

24

thought that the partnership foundation which would be needed for Uíbh Ráthach was recognised and provided for by the state also. It was expected that this would be reflected in the funding mechanisms implemented by the government bodies.

It was hoped to find a quicker and more assured way to agree on a budget because of all the developments in communication.

Things turned out differently however. That was made clear to Comhchoiste as the funding consequences of the Irish sub-plan were being worked out after the launch of the development plan. In this case, a lot of time and energy was invested, not only during the planning process but again after the launch of the plan. Comhchoiste sought funding from the outset for the three years of the plan and again at the later stage when a cohesive reporting formula was being discussed.

During all this time Údarás na Gaeltachta had a very deep understanding of what the Comhchoiste wanted to achieve and gave every possible help to resolve the issues. As a result of these discussions the difficulties in getting funding for 2006 were not significant. Unfortunately, the same certainty of funding did not apply to the 2004 – 2005 budget. This had a crucial effect in breaking the continuity of the work plan during those years.

On a positive note, the main lesson that the Comhchoiste has learned is that development plans should be kept simple. Critically a co-ordinated and comprehensive view is needed so that everyone participating clearly understands every objective which is agreed and in place. That said, another step needs to be taken at that point to separate the objectives from each other once again and to present them to each organisation in simple format. Essentially it appears easier for the state to deal with small plans instead of one big plan containing different levels.

Now as we begin the third year of the plan the Comhchoiste is reasonably happy with the progress made in the plan's objectives. Some items are still without funding and as a result have not yet begun. We are up to date with the funded items. Soon we will review the whole plan with the help of an independent facilitator. This will re-inspire the committee and the staff for the best use of the time remaining until the plan ends.

Reflections

There is no doubt that in relation to Irish, the future of Uíbh Ráthach depends greatly on the language sub-plan of the Comhchoiste. In 1999 Coláiste na Sceilge in Cathair Saidhbhín was opened as an All-Irish Unit which for the first time ever serves the educational post-primary needs of Uíbh Ráthach Gaeltacht. It is the philosophy of the Comhchoiste that the whole of the peninsula should be viewed, both Gaeltacht and Galltacht together, as a natural linguistic entity. There are difficulties certainly with this philosophy, especially on a practical level. It is difficult for the committee to properly serve the whole peninsula not to mention the Gaeltacht area which is so dispersed but it is a necessary approach.

Without Irish medium post-primary education this Gaeltacht will not survive. At the same time, for population reasons mainly, that particular education service will not survive without support from areas outside the Gaeltacht boundary. Because of this the Comhchoiste has appointed a Language Assistant and a Youth Officer which are funded by Foras na Gaeilge and those staff members are working outside the Gaeltacht. It is an encouraging sign for the peninsula to see the continual and substantial increase of pupils attending the All-Irish Unit in Coláiste na Sceilge.

However, this approach (i.e. promoting Irish outside the Gaeltacht boundary) is not completely free from problems. It is very difficult to secure funding for particular schemes which are essential within the Gaeltacht because some funding agencies feel that the resources are available to the Comhchoiste already. Because of the obstacles that relate to grants from various organisations, resources funded by Gaeltacht bodies like Roinn na Gaeltachta or Údarás na Gaeltachta cannot be used outside the Gaeltacht. Likewise, in the case of Foras na Gaeilge, funding cannot be used within the Gaeltacht. The result is that currently in the case of the Comhchoiste we do not have the Youth Officer or the Irish Assistant working within the Gaeltacht. It is difficult to explain that problem to the Gaeltacht funding bodies. There are strict funding rules in force and they conflict with the philosophy of the Comhchoiste, but we have no choice but to be happy with them and to work with them.

From 2004 the Heritage Officer has undertaken the duty of Language Planning. Amongst the many Comhchoiste schemes, there is a home support initiative. This is considered the most important aspect of the Language Plan. This scheme is for families who have a need for practical support for the whole family whilst the children are being reared with Irish. The Comhchoiste knows how vitally important these families are for the future of the Irish in the Gaeltacht. The scheme is progressing very well even though the funding is limited. The Gaeltacht parents are demanding aid and the Comhchoiste hopes to develop and increase the home support scheme. We cannot depend on the Naíonraí (pre-schools) and the education system to inspire children to speak Irish – this must come from the parents themselves.

In addition there is a FETAC (Further Education) course 'Raising Children with Irish' being run in the area and it is well attended. There is a language speaking group and Irish classes for every level provided for by the Irish teacher. Last year the Comhchoiste began a Diploma in Irish in conjunction with University College Galway.

Nearly every level of ability is being catered for through Irish now – from achieving a third level qualification in Irish to the complete beginner. What is most remarkable about this education service is that this is the first time that people have it on their doorstep. We also organise social events like heritage festivals and musical nights which give people an opportunity to this small Gaeltacht community to converse in Irish and meet socially.

The progress made in six or seven years is immense. This is especially so when the present situation is compared to the dark years of the 1980s. Uíbh Ráthach has achieved recognition as a Gaeltacht and the area is represented on regional and county committees. Programmes from the area are regularly broadcast on Raidió na Gaeltachta. The Comhchoiste has issued compact discs and publications which celebrate the heritage and genius of the area. Comhchoiste has won many development awards and the smaller committees connected to the Comhchoiste have won Glór na nGael, Gníomh don Ghaeltacht (Action for the Gaeltacht) and An Baile Beo (Living Town) prizes. These could all be considered small steps but they cannot be underestimated with regard to the inspiration that they give to a weak Gaeltacht area like Uíbh Ráthach, a Gaeltacht community which that was left marginalised for long enough but which is now presenting itself on the big stage where the community is celebrating anew its own identity.

The future

There is no doubt that Uíbh Ráthach has turned a corner. There is a sense of new growth in the area. The people are alive again, they know that the Gaeltacht status is in danger, they realise that they are to blame if it is lost, they understand how valuable Irish is and that it is worth protecting and nurturing. But more than anything, for the first time ever, the community of Uíbh Ráthach Gaeltacht know that there is support, guidance and help available to them to hold on to this beautiful gem,their inheritance from their elders.

A history of Irish language development in Carlow since 1970

Bríde de Róiste

History and background

Many people have endeavoured to promote the Irish language in Carlow since the first Glór na nGael committee was established in the town in 1970 – the same year that I arrived from West Clare to live by the Barrow as a young, newly qualified teacher.

According to the minutes recorded by the secretary, Pádraig P. Ó Drisceoil, 'Glór na nGael was established in Carlow when Father Tomás Ó Fiaich spoke about the aims and objectives of the competition at a public meeting which was convened in the Royal Hotel on the 27th of April 1970. It was attended by two hundred people, both young and old'. The minutes also provide a description of the spirit and fervour of the committee and the speed with which it did its utmost to win a prize – which it succeeded in doing when Carlow was presented with a Certificate of High Commendation in the National Glór na nGael Competition, 1970.

As I have said, since then many people – hundreds doubtless – year after year have been connected to some extent with the world of the Irish language here in Carlow Town.

I attended my first meeting of Glór na nGael in the Crofton Hotel on the 11th of February 1973 but really it was a case of Máire and Séamas Mac Páirc taking me there. At that particular time the Irish language was in a poor state in Carlow and the efforts of Irish speakers to impress the ordinary public were largely ineffective. To tell the truth there had been a decline in the Irish language in the area and a small group of enthusiasts came together to mount a new attempt for the cause. Among those enthusiasts was Father Caomhín Ó Néill, Deirdre Mhic Bhranáin, Séamas Mac Páirc, Pádraig Ó Snodaigh and me. The vision we all had was to build respect for the Irish language, art and culture generally among the ordinary local people, young and old. It was evident to all that the general attitude to the Irish language in Carlow during the seventies was of a boring school subject that was useless, unimportant and had no function outside the classroom.

29

Reflections

It was clear to us that it was not worthwhile to organise heavy, academic occasions or events because they would not attract the ordinary people. Therefore, we constructed the pathway to bilingualism and opened the back door to the Irish language in Carlow.

We decided to organise a weekend of events which would encourage those with very little Irish rather than target the small group of Irish speakers. That is how Éigse Cheatharlach was founded in April 1979. There was an art and craft exhibition, a wine and cheese party, a céilí, a walk, poetry reading, the Éigse race, an outdoor concert, a cultural parade and Father Pádraig Ó Fiannachta on a lorry on the Athy Road to officially open Féile na hÉigse.

We were very proud and happy with ourselves when the crowds came out to all the Éigse events from Friday to Sunday. An Irish atmosphere with a new spirit and a positive attitude to Irish could be felt throughout the town during the whole weekend. For the first time ever there was a festival in Carlow and, better again, it was organised by Irish speakers. Support for the Éigse came from every level of society – the local authorities, the local newspaper The Carlow Nationalist, business people, the schools, the church and the local people. Unconditional generous support for the festival with the strange name – the most common question was "What does Éigse mean?" That was a significant change from the question that had previously been on everyone's lips – "What is the point of Irish, why have it at all?"

It was evident that a new era was beginning in Carlow in relation to the Irish language. We in Glór na nGael decided to seize the opportunity and emphasise the teaching of Irish to young children. I personally had a very simple vision which was shared by all the members of the committee. That was to begin teaching Irish in a simple, natural way that was fun and enjoyable. Then we heard about the pre-school movement and the Comhchoiste Réamhscolaíochta. People such as Aingeal Ó Buachalla, Helen Ó Murchú and Máire Uí Ainín from the Comhchoiste visited us and the first pre-school was established in Carlow, under the aegis of the Comhchoiste Réamhscolaíochta, in 1980. Our loyal friend, Treasa Uí Thuathail, who passed away on St. Patrick's Day 1997, was in charge of the pre-school.

It was not long before the parents of the children in the pre-school agreed with the members of the committee that there was an urgent necessity for the establishment of a primary school in Carlow or the effect of the pre-school would be lost. Following a very short campaign, and with the help of the renowned broadcaster, Mícheál O Muircheartaigh, and the County Manager, Mícheál Ó Buadhaigh, Gaelscoil Eoghain Uí Thuairisc was established in September 1982.

As naturally as the life of the pupil going from stage to stage, we realised quickly that our vision for Carlow was not complete until we would provide for second level education through Irish. And that is exactly what happened with the support of the VEC (Vocational Education Committee) and great help from Máire Uí Ruairc, TD, who was the Minister for Education at the time. Gaelcholáiste Cheatharlach was established on the 1st of September 1990.

So at last there were, are and will be fluent speakers for the next generation provided by Naíonra Ceatharlach, Gaelscoil Ceatharlach and Gaelcholáiste Ceatharlach. A Dream – A Vision – call it what you will but we have it in abundance now!

Education is not enough, however, and side by side with the development of completely Irish medium education we also understood the pressing need for the creation of facilities for social life, pastimes and entertainment events to cater for the pupils, their parents, and – most importantly – for those amongst the ordinary public who had no connection to education or any school. With the help of the post-primary Irish teachers, Déaglán Ó Bric, Seán Ó Ceallaigh and Siobhán Uí Roibeáird, we decided to establish a club for the teenagers of the town where they could enjoy each other's company through the medium of Irish. Club Dhéagóirí na Dolmaine was founded, with and for teenagers, and they had great craic every Friday and Saturday evening. Who would have thought there would be a membership of 200 in the club, and a waiting list. And why? Well, that was the time when there were no part-time jobs for teenagers and they were not attracted by the disco or drink. Indeed no, but Déagóirí na Dolmaine gave the boys and girls an opportunity to meet each other, play board games, prepare sketches and plays for the stage, swing each other inIrish dances such as The Walls of Limerick and Ionsaí na hInse, go on trips as far away as Connemara. Didn't they have the life of it! Wasn't it worth their while to speak Irish!

The parents were also very happy because they trusted those in charge of the teenagers. The pupils had a safe and healthy social life along with an opportunity to improve their Irish. Those were the days.

Thirty years ago there was little traditional music to be heard in Carlow and when we decided to start an informal session every Monday evening in the Oaklands Hotel good traditional musicians were motivated to come out and play in public. Believe it or not, the same session continues to this day every Monday evening in the same hotel. With sessions starting in many pubs and a weekly Céilí in the Carlow Lodge Hotel, along with top class concerts from famous musicians and groups such as Dé Danann, Altan, Na Casadaigh, Stockton's Wing and plenty of others, we succeeded in sharing the musical tradition with the local people, and that is continued still by the strong active committee of Comhaltas Ceoltóirí Cheatharlach.

What helped us in impressing the public? Well, if I had to choose one thing which helped with the growth and revival of the Irish language in Carlow I would have to be very honest and mention this – we were beginning at a very basic level in a large town. Carlow did not have much of a reputation. There was not a festival or an active organisation worth talking about in the town. I thought the people of the town were hungry for something – anything that would add enjoyment, hope and courage to their lives and hearts – anything unusual… A Fair, A Festival, A Pre-school, A Club, A Parade. Anything at the time would have succeeded. My fellow committee members and I were very lucky that we were in the right place at the right time. Support and good will came from every section of the community – the business people, the church, the local authorities, teachers and schools. Suddenly the Irish language and everything connected to it had a central position in Carlow – a garrison town that had once been inside the area of the Pale, a complete transformation from a town of foreigners to the winners of the National Glór na nGael prize in 1982 and again in 1995. Who would have believed back in 1970, when Father Tomás Ó Fiaich spoke at the inaugural meeting of Glór na nGael in the Royal Hotel, that this could happen? Life is often strange.

The current situation

I have no doubt that the Irish language and everything connected to it is in good shape in Carlow Town at present. It is fine to initiate various events but it is a different thing altogether to invest in and perpetuate the different aspects of any organisation to ensure that it is not merely a one day wonder. That is how the Irish language is in Carlow, in relation to our fully Irish educational institutions in particular.

This cannot be denied when you see three pre-schools operating in the morning and evening with a qualified staff of eight employed in them to give the best of care to the children. Add to this the growth and development of the Gaelscoil from twenty children and one teacher in 1980 to 470 pupils now with twenty teachers on the staff. Add to that Gaelcholáiste Cheatharlach with 230 pupils and twenty teachers providing the best of second level education.

After spending years in prefabricated rooms for both teachers and pupils, it is a cause of great joy and celebration to us that beautiful new buildings costing ten million euro are presently (late 2005) in the process of construction by the Department of Education and Science as permanent accommodation for the Gaelscoil and the Gaelcholáiste. That is a sign of confidence in the Irish language in Carlow ahead to the next generation and the next century. The spoken language, although it is not as widely used by the community as we would like, has definitely reached a new level in Carlow.

There is a particular understanding here of the importance of Irish and the culture that goes with it. This is true in many facets of life. Many organisations and clubs are working to focus the attention of the community on our culture, our heritage and, of course, on our language itself. There is a Gaelic disposition flourishing among the Carlow community, with every section of society and all age groups having respect for the movement and the new era for the Irish language under the leadership of Glór na nGael.

The locally based media are chasing stories of hope in relation to Irish day after day. Among them are The Carlow Nationalist and The Carlow People, not to mention the local radio station KCLRFM. The local authorities and business people understand that the Glór na nGael committee welcomes any new challenges and projects so grants of aid are enthusiastically and generously made without their even being applied for. One need only mention the St. Patrick's Day Parade, the Harvest Festival and the new bilingual advertisements scheme recently announced by the Minister for Community, Rural and Gaeltacht Affairs. Carlow Town Council have made €6,500 available for the advertising scheme in its estimates for this year (2006). That is trust and confidence in the Irish language and those involved in it of a kind which did not exist in Carlow thirty years ago.

Reflections

The future

I have done enough looking back so I will now look to the road ahead. There is still the same vision and hope regarding the Irish language in the air in Carlow. It is still my aim to have the language in centre stage in relation to everything that is taking place, and will take place, in the Carlow community. One thing that will add a lot to the promotion of Irish in Carlow, and had been scarce enough until now, is the large choice of fluent speakers available to discuss any subject. Our students have gone through the education system here already – doctors, artists, scientists, journalists, teachers, graduates in every subjects.

With the number of ex-students from Gaelscoil Cheatharlach and Gaelcholáiste Cheatharlach always increasing, Carlow will have the solution to the biggest obstacle to the development of Irish until now – that is the ability to speak the language fluently and naturally without stress, trouble or pressure. The cúpla focal (few words) is no longer any use in Carlow. Goodwill is not enough either. In order to be able to serve the community properly in the future the appropriate person will have to be found to attend to whichever need arises through the medium of Irish as well as it is done through the medium of the English language. There will be no place for pretence in the future and it will not be accepted in the Irish language community. Let us always be professional.

If there is one other chapter we can add to the educational sphere in Carlow, what I would really like to see is the step to third level being taken. And perhaps the idea is not so fanciful. Does Carlow not already have two colleges - The Technology Institute and Carlow College which was once a seminary for student priests. The students already have Irish as an optional subject on the degree course and there is a diploma in Irish in conjunction with Galway College University being followed by twenty mature students. I can envisage Carlow College as a Training College for primary school teachers sooner or later. It would be a wonderful service, because there is an urgent need for the best of fluent teachers newly trained to fill all the vacancies that will arise in the Irish schools of the country in the future.

Why have the Training College located in Carlow? Well, why not?

I think that the Irish language revival in Carlow will not be totally successful in the future until there is someone employed as an organiser to guide the

34

movement professionally. There has been too great a change in the life of the individual and of the family to depend entirely on voluntary work. This person should also be available to do the work of Glór na nGael during the working day, when the business world is operating, rather than assume that arrangements made at meetings and voluntary work at night when all the offices are closed are enough. I am thinking of a Glór na nGael officer to spread the language throughout the county as well as Carlow Town ... and it would not be a Gaelic Officer who spends all his time at paperwork, forms, translations and County Council office work. If I were to win the lottery, or if an appropriate grant was made available, I would spend it on this because I think it would be a great sin if all that has been achieved by voluntary committees in relation to Irish were lost because the voluntary worker is no longer available.

I agree entirely that young people are central to the revival of the language if it is to survive into the next generation. I also agree that the family has a particular place in the movement. To that end we are creating a lot of opportunities to ensure many worthwhile and enjoyable activities for children and families. The establishment of a branch of COMHLUADAR (for families) here in 2005 is a step forward. A wonderful committee has been established, encouraging other young families to actively participate in the organisation. I expect that this will continue until Irish is the family language.

There are many regular events taking place throughout the year such as sports courses, youth club and a summer camp through the medium of Irish in July. All the events are well attended. Young people have a big input to the Irish Mass in the Cathedral, serving on the altar, reading the lessons and as members of the choir.

Talking about the Mass, I can say that Irish is well supported in church affais and has been since the beginning. There is a Mass in the Cathedral on Saturday evening performed by the clergy in the parish. All the sacraments from baptism to marriage are made available through Irish as well as the provision of a chaplain for the Irish schools. This is no small contribution and we are grateful for the support and recognition from the Bishop and clergy.

We organise very enjoyable events and festivals throughout the year which are well supported by the community. During the early years the people talked about Éigse Cheatharlach whereas now they ask for a Seachtain na Gaeilge (Irish

Week) programme, not to mention the Harvest Festival which has taken place each autumn for the past thirteen years. With the local authorities, the local media – both print and broadcast, business people, organisations such as the CCÉ (which promotes Irish music), GAA (the Gaelic Athletic Association), Archaeological Association, constantly supporting the aims and objects of Glór na nGael it is clear that the organisation is having an impact on the community. Add to that the large number of people who are working in the field of Irish and the picture of Irish affairs in Carlow now and for the future is a healthy one. Irish, and everything associated with it, is fashionable and modern. May it remain so for a long time to come.

Conclusion

I can personally say that I have been lucky to have been present while this wonderful progress has been happening in Carlow. I do not think there will ever again be the same kind of growth and development in the town. There certainly was a lot of work, time and trouble involved in the effort but there was also pleasure, satisfaction and, yes, pride, associated with it sometimes!

I thank the community in Carlow generally from the bottom of my heart, but I particularly want to thank all those who participated with me in organising every kind of event over the years. If not for these people, many of whom have passed away, my own efforts would not have borne fruit, neither would there be any talk of the turnaround in the fortunes of Irish in Carlow today. Long life to those who are working in Irish today, and good luck to all your efforts.

GLOR - Gaeilge Locha Riach

Eoghan Mac Cormaic

Background and history

A small country town or a large region: which of these best describes the focus of the local committee known as GLOR, Gaeilge Locha Riach? It is worth asking that question so that the reader might understand the work of the committee and the state of Irish in the community with which the committee is working.

Loughrea is situated about 40 kilometres east of the city of Galway roughly halfway to Ballinasloe on the main N6 road to Dublin. The town is rapidly expanding, just as many other towns are experiencing growth and undergoing changes in community habits of travel, work and background. When the work of GLOR began at the end of 1999 the town had a population of around 3500 but in the years since then more than 600 new houses have been built in the town, while the surrounding countryside is also becoming urbanised.

There is not a great tradition of Irish in Loughrea although it is said that there were native speakers here until the 1930s and even later in the Sliabh Aughty mountains just south west of Loughrea. Indeed in the 1930s a local schoolmaster, Seán Ó Flannagáin, carried out a folklore collection in the area. A large part of this collection was published in 2005 in a book titled Glórtha Ár Sinsear, edited by Pádraig Ó Baoill.

I moved to Loughrea in 1999 when my wife and I bought a house halfway between Loughrea and the town of Gort. From the beginning much of our business was in Loughrea, and as it happened I knew some of the local Gaeilgeoirí through Conradh na Gaeilge. Just before moving to Loughrea I taught Irish classes to children and adults in a ten week course organised by the local Craobh (branch).

Reflections

I had been a member of Conradh na Gaeilge in Galway since 1991 when I came to the west to go to UCG (University College Galway), now NUIG (National University of Ireland, Galway). Through Conradh na Gaeilge I met with Pádraig Ó Baoill, a language activist married and living near Loughrea. Pádraig was a member of the local Craobh and I knew from him that Conradh had spent some time in recent years trying to re-organise this Craobh and others in the south Galway area. Some of these Craobhacha in County Galway were in a weak state; sometimes the Craobh consisted of older Gaeilgeoirí and often with members who had neither the time nor the energy which they once had for language promotion. In Loughrea the problem was a lack of members but the Craobh had potential.

I attended the AGM of the local Craobh at the end of 1999. The meeting was taken up with the usual reports: organising classes, attending meetings of the Craobh, attending meetings of the Coiste Dúiche (the Regional Committee of Conradh na Gaeilge), the St Patrick's Day collection and so on. The meeting had other business to attend to, however, and, of the four or five present, people spoke of their plans to protect the townland names in the area, to lobby developers to use Irish language names for new estates, to open a naíonra (pre-school).... and by the look of things they were serious and believed that they could achieve all this. When the elections for the officer board were taking place I was proposed as Cathaoirleach (Chairperson). This of course is a tried and tested trick which many Irish organisations use - of presenting the last person into the room with a job. However I was interested in promoting the language and I respected people like Declan Shaughnessy and Pól Mag Lionáin who were present and willing to share their thoughts with the meeting. I agreed to become Cathaoirleach (Chairperson) on the basis that we would have another meeting to draw up a comprehensive plan of work.

Thinking back to that period now I ask myself what was the target, or indeed targets, of those who drew up the plan of work. A love of the language and a desire to see more people using it was obviously a common thread, Some of us were also parents with young children – one parent already had children in school but was looking for help with their Irish. In the case of Pádraig Ó Baoill and myself our children were still very young and we were looking at the possibility of all-Irish schooling for them.

The Craobh began drawing up some objectives. We put together a wish list: to employ someone full time in language work, to open a naíonra, to establish a gaelscoil, to have Irish language signage in local shops, to have a regular Irish language publication, to have Irish language names chosen for any new estates, to open an Irish language youth club etc. We were also hoping to increase the number of Irish language events being organised in the town even if we were starting from a very low level. We also knew that we could not see the whole picture, so we agreed to carry out a language survey of Loughrea to assess the opinions and needs of the town.

Pádraig Ó Baoill contacted the Gaelscoileanna office in Dublin looking for advice on the opening of a new school. In hindsight we knew very little about the system. Both Pádraig and myself are from the north and we were trying, no doubt, to use northern methods, (which evolved from the particular conditions there) in Loughrea (which had different conditions). Even in small things like terminology, where we would be speaking of naíscoil and bunscoil and others would be using naíonra and gaelscoil it took time to adapt. We were also, as it happened, very innocent as to the level of opposition we were to meet from the system, from the Catholic church and other interest groups.

When we organised our first public meeting about the gaelscoil in November 1999 there were more representatives present from the organisation Gaelscoileanna than parents! The Gaelscoileanna representatives advised us that we would need to put our application in before the end of December and that we would need 17 names. A fortnight later we held our second public meeting but this time we advertised it as a meeting about the new gaelscoil which was opening in September 2000. That meeting was attended by 20 parents and we enrolled enough at the meeting to put in our application. We had learned a valuable lesson about 'positive spin'.

As we started work preparing for the opening of the school, it became clear that there are a lot of different Irish language organisations, some of which I had never heard of, and others of which I had no idea of the roles they played. There was a level of co-operation between them at local level, and between their timirí (local organisers) and development workers. Someone would arrive out to us from, say, Gaelscoileanna and suggest that we meet with someone from the Foras Pátrúnachta (a company established to act as Patron for some gaelscoileanna). Via Conradh na Gaeilge we were put in touch with the pre-school organisation Chomhchoiste Réamhscolaíochta or Forbairt Naíonraí Teo. Someone else pointed us in the direction of Glór na nGael and from there we tied into the County Council Irish Officer. We were like serial Gaeilgeoirí building up, and tying into a support network for our plans. It is worth repeating that we received help from individuals and from organisations, and that there were days when that help was needed.

In the year 2000 we opened Gaelscoil Riabhach, a very lively, democratic and open school. There is nothing 'wonderful' about opening a school but what is wonderful is to see a school growing and surviving. We had a number of parents (with very little Irish it must be said) who put their hearts into the school from the beginning. They could always be relied on for collections, for discussing the school's vision and more that anything else for spreading the gospel and finding children to enroll year after year. By the time the school opened its door for its first pupils the Craobh had already begun working on another item on the agenda: research.

During the first six months of 2000 a member of the Craobh began working on a FÁS Education and Training scheme through Conradh na Gaeilge in Galway. He went from door to door round every house in Loughrea carrying out a survey. The detailed questionnaire had been drawn up during our regular meetings – often meeting two and three times a week during those months. The survey covered every aspect we could think of which related to Irish: classes, education, pre-school, support for Irish, signage in shops, estate names etc.

When all the forms had been collected we studied them and published them in booklet form at the end of 2000. Although some of us were by now members of the Board of Management of Gaelscoil Riabhach we were looking for new members to manage the naíonra and to be members of the naíonra committee independent of the Craobh. In early 2001 we felt that we were in a strong enough position to organise a major conference in east Galway and we succeeded in getting funding from Foras na Gaeilge to assist with that. In September 2001 the naíonra 'Tigh na Sí' opened and GLOR opened its first office to the public with the assistance of the funding from Foras na Gaeilge.

The conference was a success, bringing representatives from many different groups together and much was discussed and debated during the workshops. People from different groups made contacts and GLOR was able to showcase all that had been achieved to date. However by the end of the day it was clear that to keep up the momentum and to deal with the new tasks and ideas arising from the conference that a full time worker would be needed.

We knocked at the door of Foras an Gaeilge again and were promised a grant for the year 2002.
There is no doubt that a full time post helps to complete tasks but it must also be said from our experience that the success of having a full time development worker relies on having a good working committee. I applied for and was employed as the Development Officer with GLOR at the beginning of 2002 on a one year contract. In the absence of any clearer definition of the job I took it that I was employed by GLOR and available to any Irish language organisation or scheme in the town and in the surrounding district. Just as the local Craobh had broadened its role from organiser of classes to one of establishing a school and naíonra, so now did GLOR expand its focus from a small rural town to a far wider area.

Looking back now I believe that the participation of the Craobh began to reduce as the role of GLOR and the independent committees increased. A school management committee is a statutory body with specific duties. A Naíonra steering committee is independent and is elected annually. Committees like these eventually develop their own vision which may not always be the same as the vision first conceived by the founding committee. In addition a full time development worker is working in the field so to speak and cannot always follow an original script.

Even today I cannot say with certainty that the vision and plans of the Gaeilgeoirí have been fully accepted by all the people of the town. Many families are now relying on the gaelscoil for their children's education (and indeed both the gaelscoil and the naíonra have waiting lists at the time of writing). Some families understand that there is more to the package than the school alone. Some families have supported our Irish language summer camps (running every year since 2001) and by attending and supporting our events during Seachtain na Gaeilge etc. However the majority of parents here who have chosen a gaelscoil for their children do not place the same importance on securing other services through Irish... they will battle away for the success of the school but they would not have the same interest in Irish per se.

One example of this is preparation for First Communion. The First Communion became a contentious matter in the early days of the school. This had implications for other aspects of Irish beyond the school gates.

Gaelscoil Riabhach is a multi-denominational school. Some parents in the school wanted the sacraments for their children and so a Catholic Parents Committee was formed. This committee pays for a teacher to teach religion after school. While the organisation of any religious classes is not the business of the school the Board of Management facilitates the use of classrooms after school for religion or First Communion classes. One would imagine that this arrangement would be straightforward but unfortunately it did not suit other interest groups.

The parents choice to make Gaelscoil Riabhach a multi-denominational school meant that it would be recognised for ever as independent of any church control. The arrival of the gaelscoil offered parents a choice: Irish language education instead of English language as in other schools in the town; co-educational instead of divided into boys and girls as in other primary schools in the town and multi-denominational and independent from the Catholic church unlike the other schools in town. (Like many other small Irish towns, Loughrea does not have a Protestant school). I suppose this can only have been seen as a challenge by some to the power of the old order.

Rumours began circulating that the IRA and Sinn Féin were behind the school – indeed there are probably some in the town who still believe that. For example in 2005 when GLOR began a campaign to open another gaelscoil in the nearby town of Athenry I received a telephone call one evening from a prospective parent asking if it was true that Sinn Féin would be collecting money from the school!

As those rumours began to abate other stories began circulating in Loughrea that parents would have to pay huge fees in this 'private school'. And then came the story that the parish priest was refusing to recognise teaching and preparation for First Communion. Of course we persisted and overcame every hurdle but there is no doubt that we lost children because of the rumours. The animosity spread out to cover Conradh na Gaeilge and the naíonra too, as neither group were allowed space in the parish bulletin to advertise their existence. Even today there is little co-operation between that side of the town and the Irish language organisations.

As I have already mentioned we began creating links with other groups and competitions back in 1999-2000. The committee registered with Glór na nGael and in the first year we were adjudicated we won three prizes. Two years later we won another prize and in 2005 the committee moved up to Level 4 (although we realise that we still have a lot to do to win the competition).

As part of our original Fís Ghaelach (or Vision for the Irish language) in 1999 the Craobh understood that we would need to cover every aspect of life from pre-school to adulthood. One of our catchwords at the time was that if it was available in English we would make it available in Irish. By the time we had three or four separate committees functioning, the Development Officer employed and the GLOR offices open, it was important too to co-ordinate between the groups to ensure that the same work was not being duplicated, and that each group could cross-support the work of others. The was particularly noticeable in events during Seachtain na Gaeilge and in the summer camps.

The current situation

During the lifetime of GLOR to date I believe that many aspects of Irish life have been covered. Among the projects we managed were: two annual summer camps in both Loughrea and in Gort; a film club on Saturday mornings for 7-14 year olds with Ógras; a Comhluadar (family) group which held events, workshops, picnics and Christmas parties; a Treasure

Hunt as part of Heritage Week; publishing books, calendars and newsletters; poetry competitions; shop window competitions; sponsorship of Irish language signage; schools competitions – essays and art; daytime, evening and intensive weekend Irish courses for children, adults and the Leaving and Junior Certificate examinations; Seachtain na Gaeilge, a gaelscoil in Loughrea and both a primary (Gaelscoil Riada) and a secondary (Coláiste an Eachréidhe) opening in Athenry in 2006.

I began this article with a question about the range of work of the committee, posing the question as to whether our work covered a town or an area. GLOR was not long in existence when we began to shift the focus to other parts of the county. Every area has its own way of doing things and so we needed to be careful that we always brought the local people with us in any new project we were starting. One example of this was the campaign to open a new secondary school in East Galway. I organised the first public meeting for the school in Loughrea in February 2004 and in the following two years the committee moved its meetings from town to town thus ensuring that we had representation from all the gaelscoileanna in the wider area. When the committee finally chose a location for the school it opted for a central location, thus ensuring that there would not be the perception of any one school having an advantage over the rest.

From the beginning Glór has relied on funding from Foras na Gaeilge. It would be difficult for a local committee to come up with the finances to pay for wages, rent etc under its own steam. While some of the work of GLOR could be done on a voluntary basis (and indeed much voluntary work still continues), without a fulltime person a lot of the co-ordination and co-operation would not happen. The same can also be said about building contacts with statutory bodies such as the County Council, Town Council, Government Departments etc. The committee is grateful for all the help received but it was difficult for us to understand the cutbacks in funding which took place at the end of 2004, not only in GLOR's grant but for other projects all across the country. At the very time that our workload was increasing, when the committee was expanding to other areas, when visible results were there of the benefits coming from Foras funding, that period of cutbacks and tension damaged the committee's confidence in Foras na Gaeilge.

However we moved on, redrafting our plan of work, seeking out new sources of funding and finding new members to assist with the voluntary work. Judging by the latest annual report written by Pádraig Ó Baoill (who is now employed as Development Officer) it is clear that he has found new energy and drive in the work of GLOR. It is also coming to the point where the critical mass has been reached and that Irish is now accepted as part of the everyday life of the town. Last year, for example, when Foras na Gaeilge announced its support scheme for business signage, 70 applications were made nationally and of these 9 came from businesses in Loughrea. In the local estate agent's publicity material boasting of the advantages of living in Loughrea mention is made of the fact that the town has both a gaelscoil and a naíonra. When new housing developments are in the planning stages, the developers contact the GLOR office for advice and suggestions on names. And for the first time in the history of the local gaelscoil, there are more on the waiting list than available spaces.

That's the sort of 'problem' a committee can be comfortable with!

The future

Of course we still have to find an answer to the question, will Irish be alive in this town in ten, twenty or even fifty years. Let us look at the evidence. Six years ago there were no children in this town receiving an education through Irish. In March 2006 there were 95 in the gaelscoil and another twelve in the naíonra. By the beginning of the school year in September 2006 it was expected that the gaelscoil would have 115 and the naíonra 15 children. This year will see our first pupil leaving the school and going on to a newly opened gaelcholáiste. At the risk of overemphasising these aspects we are proud that our school welcomes children from every race, faith or social class. When we began our journey the local library had only a handful of Irish language books while now it has a shelf specifically for Irish language books for children – proof that nothing will be given until it is asked for. Irish is visible on shop signs all over the town due in no small part to a scheme organised by GLOR some years ago called Caint sa Bhaile. Demand for classes continues to grow for adults and teenagers – and we recognise that many of these teenagers have good Irish with some of them attending Summer colleges each year. The Irish language summer college for teenagers, Spleodar, deserves recognition also for the annual scholarships which it makes available locally.

In the knowledge that Irish courses and classes have their ups and downs and that circumstances can change quite quickly we nevertheless believe that we have put down solid roots now in this area. At the Christmas event organised by Comhluadar families in December 2005 there were children present from nine families. While some of the parents are not fluent speakers, they do try. They attend classes, and more importantly, they give good example to their children.

It could be said that too much has been invested in this project now to see it fail. It will not fail and all that private and personal commitment, all those visions for the future of Irish in this area, will be fulfilled. I have full confidence in the ability of GLOR to continue: we own it and we will ensure that it stays on track.

Muintir Chrónáin

Proinsias Ó hAilín

Background and history

Coiste Glór na nGael Chluain Dolcáin had been developing Irish language activities throughout the sixties in Clondalkin. On the committee were some well known names in the Irish language movement, such as the late Séamas Ó Cathasaigh, who was manager of the newspaper Inniu, and his wife Máirín Uí Chathasaigh who was also a committee member. Breandán Mac Giolla Choille – the father of Cathal Mac Coille, presenter of Morning Ireland on RTÉ, was also a member. Brother Dominic from Coláiste Pháirc Mhaoile (school) was also on the committee. Coláiste Pháirc Mhaoile would in future have an important role to play in providing facilities for the teenagers in Clondalkin. However before the end of the sixties many of the committee members of the Glór na nGael committee went their separate ways for various reasons.

It was with the arrival of the seventies that the seeds of the group we now know as Muintir Chrónáin were planted. It began in a very simple way. My wife Caitlín and myself were interested in setting up a Gaelscoil since our first son, Ruairi, was two years of age at the time. I had very little knowledge of Irish language matters in Dublin apart from the Cumann Gaelach in UCD and a few trips to the Conamara Gaeltacht during that time. My family had no Irish nor was there any tradition of Irish in the area where I grew up. I often recall hearing remarks like: *"Turn off that bloody Irish on the radio, it's giving me a headache"* when the Nuacht came on. At school you could not admit to being interested in the language or in Irish music which would be referred to as, *" awl diddly eye dye music"* .

One thing which had a great influence on me was the Christian Brothers when I was in primary school in the forties and fifties. They showed the nobility and bravery of the Gael in their tales of the Rúraíocht and Fiannaíocht. My heart would lift with pride when I heard about the land of saints and scholars or of the Book of Kells and the skill and art that lay within it. When my class was told of the role played by Irish monks during the Dark Ages, establishing centres of learning and monasteries on the continent of Europe, there was no end to my respect for my ancestors. That view of my race pleased me far more than the generally held view of the Gaeil and the people of Ireland in the forties and fifties: drunkards, dossers and worthless politicians who could not even create jobs for people. With the lack of employment and high emigration the average Irish person had very low self esteem. That contradiction between the two views of my ancestors - the school taught view and the view all around me, nourished a vision of the type of Ireland I wanted to create for my family and for my people if I could.

When Ruairi, our first child, was two years old we decided to look for Irish language education for him. Coláiste Mhuire in Parnell Square in the city centre was the nearest all-Irish school to us. We were living in the Dublin mountains, three miles south of Rathcoole. What other option had we other than to look at the possibility of establishing our own all-Irish school?

I was teaching Irish in Coláiste Pháirc Mhaoile, in Clondalkin, Dublin at the time when one day I was in the Allied Irish Bank and heard a man loudly demanding to carry out his business bilingually at the counter. I did not know him but had to ask who he was with all the commotion going on around him. Who was it only Domhnall Ó Lúbhlaí. Although I did not know him we began talking and when I found out that he was teaching in Clondalkin I knew he would be interested in the project I had in mind. When he heard what we were planning he suggested that we call a meeting with all the local Gaeilgeoirí.

We met up in Séamas Ó Cathasaigh's house in Clondalkin. Among those present at the meeting were his wife Máirín, Bríd and Éamonn Ó hÓgáin, Breandán Mac Giolla Choille, Máire and Aindrias Ó Dúill, and Domhnall Ó Lúbhlaí. The proposal was given a warm welcome although I was the only one who had a child young enough to attend a school which was not even set up yet. This however was very important in an interesting way.

In the absence of families at the meeting who had school age children Éamonn Ó hÓgáin proposed that we should cultivate a support community which would help with the campaign. This was a far more important suggestion than what we gave it credit for at the time as I will explain. Our approach was different from the approach of other Gaeilgeoirí at the time who came together to establish gaelscoileanna and who directed all their energy into a single issue, the setting up of the all-Irish school. They worked hard, they overcame their problems and a school was established, They had achieved their objective and they deserved to be satisfied. I am not suggesting that they did not continue to support the schools they had established, and many of them worked on parents committees and different groups, but the focus was on the school at all times and there is nothing wrong with that. The point that I am making is that in our case we did not focus directly on setting up a school even though that was the ultimate objective. We began by putting a support community in place. We began meeting in each others' houses. There were a few notable aspects to these early meetings. We always acted in unison. We agreed on two simple rules:

a) That we would not turn to English if someone without Irish came into the company and that it would be explained to the person that this was not due to any discourtesy but arising from a pre-agreed understanding.
b) There was a complete ban on any complaints about the government or lack of support for Irish.

Eventually the houses became too small for our meetings or indeed our social evening because there was always more to them than structured meetings. It must also be remembered that we were building a support base more than setting up a school. In any case the houses were too small for this little new community and so we decided to set forth into the outside world.

Club Chrónáin
We arranged to meet every Sunday evening in the Green Isle Hotel. We managed to attract a group of musicians and among these musicians were Muintir Dhúill, Des Carty RIP, Tom Moran, Paul Kelly, Liam Traynor and Niall Mansfield. Between music, dance, a few songs and a few pints we managed to build up a supportive community. One of the tricks we used was each Sunday we let ourselves be known to all present as a small group of people who were interested in restoring Gaelic culture including language,

music and dance in our own area. We would invite all present to use as much Irish as possible for the next five minutes and to enjoy it as much as possible. Every Irish language motivator knows that the biggest obstacle to learning Irish is the obstacle of being nervous about making a mistake.

We did well with regard to attendance and enjoyment.

One of the things which helped us was that we had a vision – to create a supportive community for Irish language education, to restore the Irish language and to open an Irish primary school in the area. We continued every Sunday in the Green Isle until the middle of the Summer and although we were happy to come back in the autumn we were asked not to return, not because of any misbehaviour. We found out later that the hotel did not want to be known as the Céilí House. Apparently this would not have fitted well with the marketing / advertising strategy which the hotel had in mind, and traditional music was not as popular then as it is now.

We were made welcome in the Belgard Inn although the only night available to us was a Wednesday. We spent a year spreading the gospel of Gaelic revival, and education and gathering a support group. At the end of that year we moved out to the John Devoy Hotel in Rathcoole.

Déagóirí Chrónáin
In the meantime there were other things happening. I set up a Club Gaeilge in Coláiste Pháirc Mhaoile, where I was teaching. Pupils from my classes used to come together to play games, for example table soccer, after school and to practise Irish. An important development from this was that a group of around forty students travelled with me to the Gaeltacht in the summer of 1973. When we returned, Déagóirí Chronáin was set up.

Coláiste Pháirc Mhaoile was a single sex school but we discovered that the girls from Coláiste Bríde were willing to take part also. Cumann na bhFiann (a youth organisation) gave a lot of assistance in the beginning and as the project developed we began to look on it as one of our most valuable assets. At its peak more that 200 members registered. Bear in mind that there was still no all-Irish school in the area but despite that spoken Irish was still very strong in the club. Structures were there to ensure spoken Irish. As a first step, applicants had to sign an application form before membership was granted. They were brought to an interview and they needed to know the words of Amhrán na bhFiann (the National Anthem) before being allowed to join. They had to sign a short contract committing themselves to speaking Irish. A system was in place to expel anyone, who - after a number of opportunities - did not keep to the commitment. Between 85 and 130 attended every Saturday evening.

If it were not for the generosity of the Marist Brothers in Páirc Mhaoile the club would not have been half as good as it was. We had the full use of the college facilities. We had out door floodlit basketball, seven table-tennis tables were available in the hall, we had a drafts league and a chess league, special interests groups, handicrafts, ju-jitsu, a tea and association room, an exercise group, a dance group and a music group. The committee used to come together at 6.45 pm to organise things and to plan the evening. The Steering Committee of the Club had a wonderful structure and composition. The usual structure was there, Committee Officers and a PRO included. But it was the teenagers themselves who steered the club. I was the only adult attending for a long while. Yet the continuity of membership kept the project going and those who left the club to move on to third level education kept the ideals of the club with them. I remember people like Bróna Ní Mhuirí, Bernadine Nic Ghiolla Phádraig, Brian Ó Gaibhín who is currently the Development Officer with Muintir Chrónáin, and Seán Ó Curráin who is now a TD (member of legislature). Bord na Gaeilge assisted by grant-aiding a PA system and various sports equipment.

The members came in at 7.30pm. The games and the groups continued until 9.00pm when a céilí would begin ending at 10.30pm. The members were very grateful to the Brothers for making their facilities available and we never had any problems with damage or misbehaviour. The drug era still had not arrived and drinking was not a problem either. One thing strengthened the club: the group who went each year to the Gaeltacht to Coláiste Bhriocáin in Rosmuc. RTÉ made two programs showing Irish language club activities for teenagers and attention was drawn to Mhuintir Chrónáin and the revival movement in the area. There is no doubt that Déagóirí Chrónáin had a huge influence on the high points which we earned in the Glór na nGael competitions in 1975 and 1978.

When Déagóirí Chrónáin came to an end it was a great loss. What happened? It was not a sudden death but a number of difficulties arose which were hard to overcome. Shortly after I was appointed as head teacher in Coláiste Chillian, a second level school which Muintir Chrónáin had set up, we lost the facilities in Páirc Mhaoile. The Club continued for a while in the Scout Hall under the direction of people like Brian Ó Gaibhín and Ruairí Ó hAilín, but with the loss of the wonderful facilities in Páirc Mhaoile it was difficult to keep up the same standards. Apart from that, other causes were calling on the resources of Muintir Chrónáin.

Óige Chrónáin

Another branch of Muintir Chrónáin had been active in another important area. Óige Chrónáin was established to work with primary school children. Once again it is worth remembering that we still had not opened an all-Irish primary school yet. Despite that, the primary level school came together every Saturday morning to play games, draw pictures and to plant the seed of Irish in the hearts of the children of the area. Mícheál Pléamoinn and Emer Nic an Bhile were responsible for Óige Chrónáin until a couple of years ago.

With all these activities going on we felt that we were attending to the needs of five important aspects of life in our society:

Óige Chrónáin focusing on the primary level.

Déagóirí focusing on teenagers.

Club Chrónáin focusing on adults.

An t-Aifreann Gaeilge (mass) which still remains strong.

Scoil Chrónáin

Returning now to Ósta John Devoy and ClubChrónáin, we met every Friday with musicians, singers, spreading the gospel, céilí-dancing – we did not know set dancing at that time. Club Chrónáin moved on to Johnstown, to Kilteely and finally came back to Clondalkin. We spent around three years in Kilteely. One of our best memories was doing a sixteen hand reel in the car park in front of the pub, by moonlight after closing time.

For various reasons the club decided to return to Clondalkin at the invitation of Cumann Peile an Chloigthí (football club) which was located in the village. It was interesting to look at the path the club had followed, starting in Clondalkin, out to the country to Johnstown in Kildare making a return journey through Kilteely and finally back in Clondalkin, all the while gathering followers and disciples. We spent thirteen years in the Club Peile every Friday evening and we were pleased to see the Irish speaking community broadening out, the speaking of Irish growing in strength and linking in with all aspects of the culture of our country. We continued with our device of drawing five minutes of Irish from all our participants. With all the broadening and strengthening it became clear that we needed our own headquarters. But first, let us return to the initial cause which brought this group of Gaeilgeoirí together at the start, to establish an all-Irish primary school.

Dónall Ó Riagáin and his wife Treasa also had an interest in securing an all-Irish education for their children. Dónall was working with Gael Linn at the time. A meeting was called for his house in Ráth Cúil in 1974 to set about the task of opening an all-Irish primary school. Dónall was a very able and highly skilled organiser. He took on the role of Chairperson of the primary school sub-committee but if he had understood the amount of hardship, tension, and slavery which lay ahead he would hardly have found the courage for it all. Opening the primary school was not the biggest challenge. In some ways that was easy enough because of the level of support coming from the work of the Club. To cut a long story short, the doors of Scoil Chrónáin opened for the first time in September 1975 in the village of Ráth Cúil. We were very lucky to have on our committee the head of Rathcoole VEC (Vocational Education Committee), the late Mícheál Ó Muineacháin, RIP. By that time the Rathcoole VEC was no longer enrolling pupils and with his help the VEC building was made available to us.

Thus began a link with the County Dublin VEC which was to prove very beneficial in the future in the development of all-Irish education. Brenda, Bean Mhic Ghinneá, was appointed Príomhoide of the new school, a very capable person who created a superb primary school whose reputation stretched throughout the county. Around a year later Naíscoil Chrónáin opened under the direction of Marie Uí Mhóráin. The naíscoil (pre-school) is still operating, under the direction of Bhróna Uí Loing.

Reflections

Coláiste Chilliain

With the passing of time the demand for post-primary Irish language education surfaced and a meeting was arranged with representatives of the VEC. We were delighted when the news came back that the VEC was willing to make the premises available for us, on Nangor Road, Clondalkin. I applied for the job of Príomhoide (Principal) and was successful. In one way I was very nervous starting in the job but in another it was the fulfilment of my dream. I remembered my primary school days and the teachers who had impressed me and the opportunity which this job now gave to me to show my pupils the type of Ireland which those teachers had shown to me. We named the new College Coláiste Chilliain. We began with fourteen pupils and by the time I took the pension in the year 2000 there were over 500 pupils on our roll books. And two other post-primary schools opened because of the demand for post-primary education through Irish in the south west of Dublin – with the credit for all that going to the staff of the college, to the support of Muintir Chrónáin, to the support of Cairde Chrónáin (Friends of Crónán) and to the support of the English and Irish medium primary schools who supplied us with pupils.

We emphasised a few things as being central to the type of post-primary education which we wanted to offer. As well as loyalty to the language we also emphasised other aspects of Irish culture, for example music, dance, field games – football and hurling. There was nothing more appealing than to listen to the sounds of the accordion, fiddle, banjo and whistle being taught while strolling along the school corridors. There was nothing more beautiful than to see the pupils enjoying céilí dancing, or the set dancers winning a trophy in some competitions, and the loyalty of the pupils to the speaking of Irish. A lot of dreams were being fulfilled, and continue to be fulfilled every day. Building the four all-Irish schools which Muintir Chrónáin opened, three of them in Clondalkin and Scoil Chrónáin in Rathcoole means that Irish is the spoken language of more than 13,000 children for most of the day. That is no small achievement for Muintir Chrónáin after 30 years.

Áras Chrónáin

I used to have an invitation for lunch with Aogán Ó Rathaille (the son of The O'Rahilly) from time to time. Aogán was learning Irish, a challenge he set himself at the age of 75. He used to invite people like Eibhlín Ní Mhurchú, Liam Ó Murchú, Síle Ní Dhonnchú and so on. I would talk about the work of Muintir Chrónáin and language revival. I mentioned that we were searching to buy a site, to build on. Next thing, he donated the orchard at the back of his house to us. An acre of land at the Newlands crossroads, for free. We had to go to the planning authorities to get planning permission, and all went well until one of the neighbours told Aogán that we intended to put a bar into the building. That was enough to put an end to the offer, because Aogán hated drink.

There was another orchard in Clondalkin, in Cusack's house on Orchard Road. It was agreed at a meeting of Muintir Chrónáin that we would approach Bert Cusack because rumour had it that he was thinking of selling the house. I came back with the good news that he was willing to sell for £200,000, which was a bargain for 2.9 acres in the middle of Clondalkin.

We had a weekly raffle prior to this to raise funds for just such an opportunity but we were well short of £200k. Des Ó Loing proposed that we should organise a raffle with tickets selling for £100. We began the work, some of us went as far as Baile Coimín and Portach Dearg in Wicklow, to Bóthar na Brúine, to Coill an Chaoi, selling the tickets and selling the dream. It is still hard to believe that people were willing to part with £100 to people that they did not know. I believe that there must be something deep inside the Gael which answers to the call of the vision of an Ireland with a Gaelic culture predominating, so long as it is defined properly. It gave me great pleasure to present the prize of a new car to someone from Portach Dearg in Wicklow, and to make £75K from the venture.

Our next venture was to make a major presentation on how we envisaged the language revival in the District of Crónán. We invited as many people from the business community as we could contact. As a result of our presentation and the generosity of people present we were not far from £100k at the end of the night. That was sufficient to go to the bank and to seek the other £100K on loan.

However we still had to spend more money. More than £150K was required to renovate the house and to satisfy the fire inspectors. Thankfully we received great assistance from the National Lottery. It would require a book in itself to describe all the voluntary work which was put into the renovation of the building, keeping in mind that this building was erected in 1835. We received help from people of all ages, trades people of every sort and all of them working voluntarily until late in the evening.

The current situation

At present Áras Chrónáin plays a central role in the Gaelic way of life not only for the people of Clondalkin but also for the people in neighbouring parishes. It is a social centre for a large number of people who love an Irish atmosphere. We have Irish music almost seven nights a week. It is also a place of learning. Irish is taught at five different levels with more than ninety people taking part in classes. There is even an Irish class now for foreign born people.

All types of musical instruments are taught with unbelievable demand for places and queues on registration night. People are turned away because of a lack of space.

There is also set dancing and céilí classes.
There is a school of solo dancing with a world-wide reputation.
There are art classes.
Instruction has been given on building a 40 foot "Bád Mór" (Boat). This arose from a suggestion by Mícheál Ó hIfearnáin as a way of encouraging members to speak Irish. The project was very successful and the Naomh Chrónáin has already made two trips to France.
We also have a very strong naíonra established by Nóra Uí Ifearnáin and which is now directed by Mháirín Uí Mhíléir.

We had to make a decision when we took possession of our own place. We felt it would be wonderful if we could implement a similar policy to Club Chonradh na Gaeilge. But we recognised that our circumstances were not the same. There weren't enough of us fluent to make it practicable and as well as that that it had always been our policy to revive Irish in a community which had little or no Irish. For that reason we decided to adopt a bilingual policy and to attack the big enemy of spoken Irish: nervousness.

This policy is going well and gradually people became used to speaking their phrases and on then to attending classes. Because of that there has been a marked increase in the amount of Irish heard and spoken in the Áras and beyond.

Looking back to that first day 32 years ago when we came together to set up an Irish language primary school in an area that had not had one for hundreds of years, and to form a support group, and to re-establish music and dance, there is no doubt that we achieved our aims. As regards schooling, not only did we open one school we opened three primary schools and a second level school.

The centre is working well. For the most part it is run on a voluntary basis. It is working so well that we had to build a new hall beside it. Eight sub-committees direct all the activities but if it was not for Risteard Ó hAllúin, who has been on the central committee for years and who shares his administration and accountancy skills generously with us, there would not be the same quality of direction or administration.

We are very lucky to have an Irish language Development Officer. Brian Ó Gaibhín has achieved a great deal since his days as Chairperson of Dhéagóirí Chrónáin and his energy and enthusiasm are limitless.

The future

Among the obstacles which remain and which are preventing us from taking a great step forward, I would include the following.

As often happens with organisations and groups like ours, a point comes when, with so much achieved, it is difficult to motivate people to move onwards to the next step. I am pleased that we have recognised that this point exists and that we are currently carrying out a major analysis of all the activities of Áras Chrónáin to meet that challenge.

We recognise that spoken Irish is not as strong among the community as we would like it to be. We are implementing a strategy to deal with this. We need to lay down the challenge to the ordinary members of Áras Chrónáin, of which there are 300, to ensure that spoken Irish is prioritised in the Áras.

Reflections

There is another community which we are also in discussion with, the teachers in the four all-Irish schools plus the Irish teachers in other neighbouring schools, to see if we can find ways of attracting them in, to be members with us.

This will strengthen spoken Irish in the Áras.

We intend to add to the number of parents whose schools use the Áras to see how many of them would be willing to be part of a campaign for spoken Irish.

Despite many attempts we are still not attending to the youth of the parish outside of the schools we established ourselves.

There is also the challenge of passing the torch on to the next generation - in other words to attract in young people who will become future activists.

We have no reason, however, to be worried and indeed the opposite is true so long as we have a clear vision and that we can bring the community along with us.

The Irish language community in south County Dublin

Brian Mac Aongusa

Background and history

'The last fortress of the British Empire in Ireland' – that is how the district that stretches through south Dublin through Dún Laoghaire to Dalkey was described during my youth. It is wonderful, therefore, that interest in the Irish language blossomed over this past fifty years in this very district. What was the cause of this phenomenon, what sort of people created it, and what sort of activities did they engage in to realise their vision? In this article I will try to answer these questions drawing on my own experience on how a heavily anglicised community transformed itself into a thriving Gaelicised community celebrating art, music, sport, social life and learning.

I was raised in an Irish speaking family by parents who had learned the language at night classes in the Dún Laoghaire technical school. Indeed, when I was young, certain old people still called Dún Laoghaire Kingstown. A shame about his lack of knowledge of his native language in a community that boasted about all things English, while denigrating anything to do with Ireland, is what motivated my father to learn Irish. My mother followed him although she had received most of her education in England. It was their vision that their children would speak Irish. The difficulties they would have to overcome would be great.

In the 30s and 40s of the twentieth century, there were only a small number of households in south Dublin in which either of the parents could speak Irish. It was among the civil servants, Gardaí, postal workers, army officers, teachers and an odd person originally from the Gaeltacht that the most Irish was to be heard. It is obvious that our parents succeeded in identifying people like themselves who were spread thinly across the district so as to develop a social life with a little Irish for their family. I remember being brought to play in the gardens of other children at the weekends, children who also spoke Irish. Often, a tram or bus journey was required to reach our play companions. It is certain that this created plenty of challenges for our parents to keep us in contact with other young children who could speak Irish. Looking back on our pre-school childhood now, I have little doubt about the importance of those visits; they showed us that we were not unique and that there were other children of our age who also spoke Irish.

When we came of school age our parents were presented with another problem. There was no school in our area that educated through the medium of Irish. There was a Department of Education Irish medium school in Dublin city centre, on Sráid Mhaoilbhríde. That school was divided into three separate parts – an Scoil Ullmhúcháin (the preparatory school), Scoil Cholmcille for boys and Scoil Mhuire for girls. There was only one other Irish medium school in Dublin, Scoil Bhríde under the stewardship of Laoise Gabhánach Ó Dufaigh. In the 40s, in the middle of the Second World War, it was too difficult to send young children on a daily seven mile journey to Dublin. Our parents therefore decided to keep us at home until we had reached the age of six and would have enough sense to make the train journey to the city centre each day. It was in the Irish medium primary school on Sráid Mhaoilbhríde that the little Irish we had blossomed. We started bringing new words and new sentences home to our own parents, which in turn added to their fluency and precision in the language. But for the trouble that our parents took to send us to an Irish medium school, it is unlikely that our interest in the language and its associated culture would ever have developed.

When we came to secondary school age our parents were presented with yet another problem. The only Irish medium secondary schooling in Dublin was in Coláiste Mhuire in Parnell Square in the north of the city, for boys only, and in Scoil Chaitríona on Eccles Street, for girls only. I was sent to Coláiste Mhuire where I took full benefit of the wide curriculum through Irish. It was not so for my two sisters as my parents were reluctant to let two young girls travel every day from south County Dublin to the north of the city. They were sent to Coláiste Chnoc Síon in Blackrock, a fine secondary school with a wide curriculum in English. But the lack of educational provision in Irish concerned our parents and others. They started thinking of practical ways to remedy the situation.

By the 1950s, our youngest brother was approaching primary school age. Life in Dublin was changing rapidly following the Second World War and our parents were uncomfortable at the prospect of sending a young boy into the city centre every day on his own. Through the network of contacts they had with other parents who were interested in Irish they started discussing the possibility of establishing an Irish medium school in Dún Laoghaire in south County Dublin. They expected that if the bunscoil succeeded there might be sufficient demand for an Irish medium secondary school later. At the start of the summer in 1951, ten parents came together to place a notice in newspapers inviting people interested in Irish medium education to attend a public meeting in the Dún Laoghaire technical college on 2 July 1951. A good mixed crowd of all classes and backgrounds turned up for the historic meeting. Great interest was expressed in the concept. A committee was established at the meeting and out of the committee's endeavours Scoil Lorcáin grew, the first Irish medium primary school established by parents for the community of their own area. The establishment and growth of Scoil Lorcáin was central to the development of the Irish speaking community in south County Dublin after that.

In early September 1952, Scoil Lorcáin opened temporarily in Blackrock Town Hall with 26 pupils registered. About one third of these had some knowledge of the Irish language already. There were two excellent teachers from Conamara - Máire Ní Chathalláin and Máire Bean Uí Chadhain - in charge. Within two months, they encouraged the natural use of the language among the other two thirds. Not only did they teach the language to the young children but they taught them the spirit of the Gaeltacht through, song, verse, story-telling, drama and sean-nós traditional singing. It was not long before it was noticed in the district that Scoil Lorcáin was no normal school. It was clear that there was an exceptional management system in the school that was greatly influenced by the parents, that the children were able to speak Irish naturally and that they enjoyed it. It was also clear that the parents were full of enthusiasm to prove that Irish medium education works and that they had set themselves the challenge of attaining high standards in every aspect of the school's activities. On account of this, a demand in the community grew among those who hitherto had no connection with anything Gaelach; people wanted their children to be part of this exceptional school that was organised through the medium of Irish.

The School Committee deepened the parents' loyalty through social events that were organised regularly throughout the school year. The committee sought the voluntary participation of as many parents as possible to help organise events such as Christmas fairs, St Patrick's Day Céilithe and Feis Lorcáin. These events inspired pupils, parents and teachers to work together regularly and to simultaneously, if unknowingly, develop their interest in the Irish language and heritage. Scoil Lorcáin grew quickly and the committee's efforts to raise money impressed on the Department of Education that there was a need for a bigger and more permanent building for the new Irish medium school. Under the direction of the committee, many events were organised to raise money, events such as coffee mornings, fashion shows, céilithe and social nights during the winters, as well as fortnight long festivals every summer. These were organised in association with Tofts or the community in general at Booterstown in Dún Laoghaire and known as Toft's Carnival & Fun Fair. Many of the Scoil Lorcáin parents worked voluntarily and diligently night after night doing the menial work of the fair in the cause of Irish medium education for their children and the district in general. As a result of their diligence in those early years, in 1957 the Department of Education gave permission to the committee to buy and refurbish Lady Dockrell's majestic house on the Belgrave Road in Monkstown, and to use it as a permanent base for Scoil Lorcáin.

The purchase of the building in Monkstown gave the parents a massive injection of confidence. It was clear that they were succeeding in realising their vision and this served to inspire them to add to their efforts to strengthen Scoil Lorcáin's standing and reputation. For the following twenty years there was a great degree of voluntary hep available from many parents to organise a wide range of events to support the school not just financially but also the teaching programme and the development of the relationships between parents, pupils and teachers outside of the school curriculum. The parents assisted the teachers in organising team training for field games, the teaching of extra subjects outside of school hours and in organising annual inter-school cultural festivals such as Feis Lorcáin which would give a public platform to the fine training that the teachers provided. These events all succeeded in bonding the parents together in one community with the sole aim of making Irish medium education of the highest standard available to their children. In the fullness of time the example of the parents of Scoil Lorcáin set other parents in the district contemplating Irish medium education. Parents in Ballinteer, Dundrum, came together with this objective in mind and before long they established Scoil Naithí, an Irish medium primary school organised like Scoil Lorcáin. As time passed, other similar gaelscoileanna grew across south, west and north Dublin, as well as in counties Wicklow, Kildare and Meath. Pupils from the gaelscoileanna began competing against each other at Feis Lorcáin and playing field games against each other, creating friendship between parents, teachers and young pupils whose lives were steeped in the Irish language. It was these events which laid the basis for the strong Irish speaking community in south Dublin.

Scoil Lorcáin succeeded as a result of the diligence of the teachers and parents over the first twenty years, a period when many people made themselves available to do voluntary work for achievable aims. Mothers of the children would work through Coiste na mBan from one end of the year to the other organising coffee and social mornings, fashion shows, Give and Take, Daddy Christmas and many other occasions to ensure a regular flow of cash for the school. Fathers of the children were prepared to spend evenings during the week and Saturday mornings working for the School Committee, overseeing football practice, adjudicating at feiseanna and assisting Coiste na mBan in organising events. Voluntary work was carried out basically to keep Scoil Lorcáin in operation when the Department of Education was not providing enough to pay the running costs of the school. But much work was also done because the parents enjoyed the camaraderie of working with others who shared the same goals and aspirations for their children's future.

It was therefore natural that a discussion developed between them about secondary level education in the area. Many wished to see Irish medium secondary schools established in the area, one for boys under the stewardship of the Christian Brothers and one for girls under the stewardship of one of the religious orders for nuns. But the parents were not all of a like mind. Some believed that Irish medium education would not be appropriate to prepare young people about to go out in the big world which was ordered completely through the medium of English. The preferred option of these parents was to send the children to one of the established English medium schools. There were nonetheless a handful of parents who firmly believed in the need to forge ahead with Irish medium education in order to ensure a holistic development for the young people who were excelling pupils in other schools because of the high quality of their education. But this group was also divided. Some were of the opinion that there would not be a sufficient enough demand to sustain Irish medium secondary education if the boys and girls did not share the same school, a proposal that would not be acceptable to all parents.

They preferred the option offered by the Dominican Sisters in Blackrock when they set up a stream for girls inside an established English medium school. Despite that, an unofficial committee of Scoil Lorcáin parents continued to lobby other religious orders in the Dún Laoghaire area to provide Irish medium secondary schooling for former pupils of Scoil Lorcáin and for other gaelscoileanna which were being established in the wider district. In the end they managed to win the agreement of the Christian Brothers and the Sisters of Mercy to establish two secondary schools in Booterstown on one campus, so that the higher classes of the two schools could come together for certain subjects for which there was not a big demand. Thus was Coláiste Eoin established under the stewardship of Brother Ó Dúgáin and Coláiste Íosagáin under the stewardship of Sister Victoire in 1975.

With the establishment of Irish medium secondary education the Irish speaking community really blossomed in south County Dublin. The foundations were laid by those parents who took the chance and sent their children to a new Irish medium school in an area where there was already a lot of established and respected schools. They were fortunate of course in that excellent head-teachers were placed in charge of the two new meánscoileanna or secondary schools, teachers who set themselves the challenge of ensuring an education of the highest standard in academic subjects, physical and personal development, leisure activities and the behaviour of the students outside of school hours. As a results of these high standards, Coláiste Eoin / Íosagáin achieved fame not just for academic excellence but also in the areas of art, music and sport. The best pupils achieved recognition in science, language, art, debating, hurling, football and basketball. Pupils in the two schools often excelled pupils from other schools in disciplines that were traditionally associated with long established English medium schools in the area.

The current situation

These high standards created self-confidence among the pupils who received their education through Irish at Coláiste Eoin / Íosagáin. Many of them continued their education to the same high standards through to third level, although at that level it was mostly through English. There can be no doubt that the pupils realised by this point that their own education was at least as good as, if not better than, pupils from English medium colleges. This understanding laid the basis for a friendship between them. They established independent initiatives with their friends who had graduated through the Irish medium sector. As a result Raidió na Life was born as was the club siamsaíochta SULT, in Dublin. It is also a fact that through these initiatives many of the multi-skilled young broadcasters have been recruited to RTÉ, TG4, TV3, Raidió na Gaeltachta and Taibhdhearc na Gaillimhe. In recent years, former pupils have also attained important positions in law, medicine, science, engineering, diplomacy and commerce in Ireland and abroad.

Looking back at what has happened in regard to Irish in south Dublin over the past fifty years, it is possible to identify a certain pattern of development. The greatest effort of the pioneers to realise their vision during the first twenty years was focused on the establishment and development of Irish medium primary education. During the second period of twenty years, from 1970 on, Irish medium secondary education was the focus. There was a good result to the efforts of parents who understood the importance of the full development of their family's education. Not only was a system of gaelscoileanna established but successful meánscoileanna were also established in the form of Coláiste Eoin/Íosagáin. Bit by bit other meánscoileanna were established – three in the west of the county at Clondalkin, Tallaght and Lucan, one in the north of the city at Swords and a further one in Bray, north County Wicklow. Today there is a network of Irish medium schools across Dublin and an unbelievable improvement on the situation that prevailed in my own youth when there was only two meánscoileanna in the city centre, Coláiste Mhuire and Scoil Chaitríona.

During the twenty years since 1990, it seems to me that the Irish speaking community in south Dublin has grown as a result of Irish medium education. Former pupils of the Irish medium schools have got to know each other in life after school through social events, while attending third level education, at music and entertainment events and through their work and professional lives. And out of these relationships projects such as Raidió na Life (an Irish language radio station in Dublin), PLÉ (a social circle in the capital city), and SULT (an entertainment initiative for young people) were established by the young people themselves. These initiatives provided much pleasure and enjoyment and added to the growth of the Irish language in Dublin.

The future

During the years to come, I believe that it will be really important to encourage contact between the former pupils of Irish medium schools, just as contact was fostered between parents and the pupils during their time attending gaelscoil. This contact is important and there are benefits to be gleaned from it for the young people, contact they should be able to develop through e-mail. It is practical information that is now needed about the opportunities which exist to participate in music, social life, the arts, science and literature. Young people who have respect for the Irish language should stay in touch with each other so as to maximise the chances of the natural growth of friendship between them, bound by the common love for our heritage in the modern world. It is worth noting, however, that the world today is not the same as it was in the 1970s and the 1980s. The high cost of living means that both parents often have to work now and people are not available to the same extent to do voluntary work as before. All the same, if young people share the common goal of promoting the Irish language then there is all the more chance they will choose to put their own children through the same Irish medium education which ensured their own success in life. If they do so, a new friendship will grow in the next generation of parents, a friendship based on a common interest in Irish medium education in a generation that will have its own ideals to achieve for families in an environment that respects the use of the Irish language.

The situation of the Irish language has completely changed in south County Dublin during the past fifty years, as have national and global attitudes. In the community in which I grew up, thanks largely to Irish medium education, a significant section of the community respect the language and its wider heritage. That is a big change since my youth when it was widely regarded that south Dublin was the last stronghold of the British Empire in Ireland.

Derry and the Irish language

Gearóid Ó hEára

Background and history

Conradh na Gaeilge was founded in Dublin in 1893 and by 1904 there were already six Craobhacha or branches in Derry.

At the beginning of the 20th Century, very few people spoke Irish in Derry. It was a Protestant city despite the majority of the population being Catholics. Most of the Catholics were originally from Tír Chonaill although they had lost their Irish some generations before that. Partition made the situation for Irish worse – the northern government was always suspicious of it and often hostile to it.

Since then there has always been a Craobh or indeed craobhacha active in the city and that small group who struggled along over the years without any facilities or official support from the northern state or the southern state kept the language cause alive. The present generation of Gaeilgeoirí is indebted to those people and, in this article, I will try to name and acknowledge some of them.

English speakers in this city used to call Irish classes 'the creeve' and there has always been a great sympathy for Irish as shown, for example, in the collections for the language. In the 1930s, there were classes in Foyle Street in Conlon's Rooms and later they moved to St Columb's Hall. At that time, the clergy in the city was closely associated with the Conradh but that weakened in the 1950s.

The late Seán Ó Canainn mentioned that he attended his first Irish class in St Columb's Hall in the 1940s, a rang (class) taken by the butcher James Doherty who had just graduated from University in Dublin. He said that he left the rang because of an over-emphasis on grammar. After that, classes were organised in a small hall in Bishop Street, where the Long Tower Primary School is today. Séan said that it was the prisoners released from internment in the 1940s who gave a new energy to Irish and he mentioned in particular the teachers from that period: Tomás Ó Mealláin, Seán Ó Cianáin, Lorcán Ó Baoill, Leon O'Timoney and

Reflections

Pádraig Ó Siadhail. These were all ex-prisoners and the same pattern remains today, working class activists and middle class academics, with a mixture of ex-prisoners, all working 'ar son na Gaeilge' (on behalf of the Irish language). The Craobh that was in existence, Craobh Cholm Cille, was in a bad state when the prisoners were released and they decided to establish a new Craobh, Craobh Sheán Uí Dhóláin, in memory of one of their comrades who had been in prison with them. They organised ranganna (classes) in Celtic Park before moving on to Bishop Street. Other people came forward as teachers and activists in the 1950s, for example Seán Ó Gallachóir, Seán Ó Canainn, Risteard Mac Gabhann and Sean Ó Siadhail who laboured away throughout the fifties from the hall in Bishop Street. At that time, there was a close link between the Irish language and the GAA (Gaelic Athletic Association) since some of these people were active in both organisations.

Things were healthy in the 1950s and in 1955 the local Craobh sought permission and a grant from Comhaltas Uladh to purchase a building known as The Sailor's Rest in Great James Street. Comhaltas rejected the request even though the Craobh had £400 of its own resources to invest. They then bought the house attached to the hall in Bishop Street. The whole premises were available to them for a while but with the re-introduction of internment in the late fifties and the removal of the main activists the organisation fell apart, factors which forced them to sell the building. That period, from the mid forties to the mid fifties, was the peak period for Irish since the beginning of the century and it is a great pity that apart from the good example, no other legacy remains.

In the sixties matters were more complex with classes being organised in different venues but a new generation was also coming through, with people like Pádaí Ó Mianáin, Breandán Ó Sandair, Proinsias Ó Mianáin, Risteard Mac Gabhann and Tomás Ó Donghaile organising ranganna and other events. They organised the Cumann Gaelach and took rooms out upstairs in the Strand Road beside the Leprechaun Bakery. They established a Drama Club and regularly entered the Oireachtas.

When I began attending classes, in the seventies, they were being organised in a hall in Bishop Street in the former BOC Club (clubrooms owned by workers from a local factory) and later they moved to upstairs rooms in Clarendon Street, possibly rooms belonging to the Inner City Trust. There were also cómhrá (conversational) sessions in the two pubs, Andy Coles and the Alleymans. However, it was difficult to maintain regular classes with regular teachers and a regular system.

Pressure began to mount in the late seventies and debates began around establishing an all-Irish primary school in Derry on the same lines as the Bunscoil in Belfast that had begun in 1972. Prisoners were coming out of the jails and, once again, they began adding to the Irish language activities in the city. There were regular meetings every Sunday in the Pilots Row Centre to discuss the establishment of the bunscoil and a club for young people. Séamas Mac Seáin and others connected to setting up bunscoileanna and the Shaw's Road Gaeltacht travelled from Belfast to speak about the difficulties they had encountered. Eventually a naíscoil or pre-school was set up. A bunscoil followed which then moved us on to a completely different level.

The current situation

Things in Derry are far healthier now that at any time over the past hundred years not only with the growth of Gaelscoileanna but also more Irish classes, schemes and Irish language events. You can now hear Irish on the streets, in the supermarket, and in the local papers, Radio Foyle and on Channel 9, the local television station. It would be difficult for a Gaeilgeoir to walk through town without meeting at least one other Gaeilgeoir. There is a Mass in Irish every Sunday and it is possible to attend the doctor, dentist, accountant, and councillor to carry out your business through Irish. There was a time when it was believed that classes were the be all and end all of language preservation but now as the language community grows and possibilities and needs arise with that growth it is clear that what is needed is community development more than language teaching. The Irish language community in Derry have set their sights higher and broader than language classes now.

Gaelscolaíocht

Since the opening of the first bunscoil in 1982, there are now five naíscoil (pre-primary), two bunscoil and a meánscoil (second level), which is organised as a stream of an English language secondary school, and there are around 450 children learning Irish annually through this system. There are also 2070 children learning Irish in the English medium schools in the city and 300 adults learning

Irish in night classes. This means that there are 2,800 learning Irish weekly in 30 venues in the city.

Naíscoil na Rinne, 1984,17 children.

Naíscoil Cholm Cille, 1984, 20 children.

Naíscoil na Gaslainne, 1987, 16 children.

Naíscoil Dhoire, 2002, 26 children.

Naíscoil Mhaol Íosa, 2003, 20 children.

Bunscoil Cholm Cille, 1983 as a stream and then as an independent school since 1993, 180 children and 9 teachers.

Gaelscoil Éadain Mhóir, 1998, interdenominational independent primary, 120 pupils and 7 teachers.

Meánscoil Choláiste Naomh Bhríde, 1995, 51 children.

English Medium Schools

Many of the English medium secondary schools offer Irish, and some of these achieve high standards and produce very capable Gaeilgeoirí. In some secondary schools, Irish is not an option until third year and by then it is too late for many pupils. A survey in 2004 estimated that 2071 pupils in English medium secondary schools take Irish.

Census 2001

In the 2001 census 162,000 or 10.4% of people in the north claimed to have some understanding of Irish. In Derry 13,808 from a population of 100,000 said that they could speak, write and read Irish. That is, 13.75% of the population of Derry.

Glór na nGael

One element that assisted the growth of Irish in Derry was the national competition, Glór na nGael. Members of the Gaeláras Irish language centre set up a Glór na nGael committee and entered the competition for the first time in 1984, winning the Best New Entry category that year.

Continuing since then, they have won:

Duais an Fháinne (prize), 1985

First Place in the Six Counties, 1989

Ulster Provincial Prize, 1991

Overall Winner, 1991 and 1999

Previous Winners Category, 1992, 1997, 2000, 2001, 2002

Participation in the competition has helped to develop a national outlook and a yardstick for progress from year to year. However, as a means of developing unity it has not worked so well.

Conradh na Gaeilge

Craobh Cholm Cille embarked on an employment scheme in 1982 from offices in Dove House in the heart of the Bogside, employing people under an ACE (Action for Community Employment) scheme and offering classes and other Irish language services. They moved to 37 Great James Street in 1988 and, in 1994, they purchased 34 Great James Street with fifteen employees taking Irish classes and involved in every aspect of the language. They bought 37 Great James Street in 2002, opening the bakery and the Caife Gaelach as well as starting every kind of Irish language event inside the building. They received planning permission in July 2005 to build a Culture, Arts and Venture Centre or Cultúrlann on the site, at a cost of £St.3.5m. Work is due to begin in Spring 2007. There are currently 22 workers in the Gaeláras participating in day and evening classes, a translation service, a book shop, café, bakery, art scheme, NUI (National University of Ireland) Galway courses, NWIFHE (North West Institute for Further and Higher Education) courses, sailing courses and a youth scheme. In the café, both learners and speakers of Irish come in to improve their command of the language. In 2005, they purchased No. 1 Queen Street to use while the other building is being re-developed.

There are a number of other groups sited in the Gaeláras:

Other groups

Droichead: Droichead (Bridge) is a cross-community group that organises talks on Irish and Gaelic culture among Protestants in the city. This dialogue has been going on for more than five years with a partnership between the Gaeláras and Epic, an organisation representing former UVF prisoners and other groups in that community. A survey on Protestant attitudes to Irish, carried out mainly by the Protestant community itself, is due for publication in 2006. Classes on Irish culture are held in Protestant areas while Epic and the Gaeláras have jointly applied for funding to employ someone from each side and to provide classes.

Gairm: Gairm (Profession) is an organisation established to provide training courses for young Irish speakers from all over the north especially secondary school leavers. A survey, funded by the northern administration, has assessed the needs of young Gaeilgeoirí and Gairm is attempting to meet the needs identified through that survey.

Doire le Dúchas: Doire le Dúchas (Derry with Native Culture) was set up in 2001 as an attempt at gaelicising Derry, from street names to roadsigns. Already there are 150 street signs erected in Irish, shops using Irish language signage, public signs in Irish and within Derry City Council a system has been established for gaelicising street signs when people request this. All internal and external signage in the City Council is bi-lingual. While Doire le Dúchas does not employ anyone, government departments have pledged funding for 2006 to employ someone to assist in establishing a Gaeltacht Quarter in the city.

Bláthanna: Bláthanna (Flowers) was established in 1998 to promote all aspects of art. The staff of three organise festivals such as - Teacht an Earraigh, Féile Lúnasa, Féile na Samhna, Scoil Shamhraidh Cholm Cille and they will organise a ten day festival around St Patrick's Day 2006. They arrange classes in set dancing, céilí and sean-nós dance, music classes in all instruments, writing and poetry classes and an annual poetry competition. They published a collection of 84 poems entitled Fís na bhFilí, in 2005, which was edited by Cathal Ó Searcaigh.

Coláiste an Phobail: Coláiste an Phobail (The People's College) organises all the courses and classes that the Gaeláras provides. There are morning, afternoon and evening classes in the Gaeláras every day while teachers also travel out to other venues including English medium primary schools to provide classes. There are classes under the aegis of NUI, Galway organised for public service employees, including the City Council, in Derry. In 2004, 28 participants received certificates at a ceremony in Galway. A partnership exists between Coláiste an Phobail and the North West Institute for Third Level Education and the University of Ulster to offer the courses that they provide, through the Gaeláras. They are currently offering a training course in computing through Irish and they will be providing traditional sailing classes on the Foyle in 2006 on a Galway Hooker, An Lady Mór, which the Gaeláras recently purchased.

Ógras: Ógras has a craobh located in the Gaeláras but it relies on funding and does not employ anyone at present, which means that the organisation of events is uneven.

Áras an Ghrianáin: Áras an Ghrianáin opened in the eighties and used to organise Irish classes, music classes and after school activities for children from the bunscoil. The Áras burned down in 2001 and some of the activities have now transferred to other venues.

Cumber House: This project, located in Cumber House in Claudy, in County Derry, is under the direction of Seán de Búrca. Cumber House provides classes, events and weekend courses on a regular basis.

Cnoc na Rós: The late Ivor Ferris approached me in 1988 with a plan to commence Irish classes in his own area of Rosemount. I introduced him to Kevin Mc Caul from the City Council and he approved a grant to start the project. Although Ivor has since passed away, his project is continuing and the group has an office in the Waterside as well as the project in Rosemount. Cumann Chnoc na Rós host five Irish classes every Tuesday evening in St Anne's Primary school as well as organising debates and courses and Irish language scholarships.

The future

Apart from the usual problems facing language revival, there are other problems also. The biggest problem facing the Irish language community in Derry is a lack of unity and, despite numerous attempts, it remains difficult to break through the parochialism and narrow-mindedness.

There may be particular reasons for the problem but generally the problem is the same today as it was in the fifties, that is that some people who are working in the sector are regarded as republicans and others who are not republicans are afraid to be connected to groups like that. This attitude has diminished somewhat with the end of the conflict and, apart from a few, most now recognise that republicans have a role to play in the Irish language movement.

Apart from that there are those who are working for the language but who refuse to co-operate with others, or who do not attend meetings and who offer specific excuses but at the end of the day, the problem is mere parochialism. Another feature of Derry is that there are many English speakers involved in the language struggle, some of whom are employed full time. In some respects, this is a positive thing but many of these people lack confidence in Irish despite years of learning and they are reluctant to attend meetings unless the meetings are in English.

Although we should keep trying to persuade people to learn Irish there are those who never will. Space must be kept for people like these, and for all English speakers, to play a part in what we are doing.

Gaeilgeoirí in this city do not have an overall strategic plan and although some groups do have plans and strategies there are other groups who do not have plans and appear unaware of the plans of others. This is evident even in groups funded by Foras na Gaeilge who do not co-operate with other groups.

Foras has a policy that groups should co-operate at all levels. Foras, therefore, has an important role in encouraging unity in this sector. Unity and a unified strategy are vital for the Irish language community in this city if we are to take Irish on to the next level. Facilities exist which we as a community are not taking advantage of, for example Irish teachers in the city who are not tied into the overall project, or receiving advice on the way forward from activists on the ground.

Work begins on the new Cultúrlann in 2006 and, when it is complete, the largest Irish centre on the island will be located in Derry city centre. It will provide a venue for a theatre, shop, café, classrooms, lecture rooms, business development units, youth space, and office space and will employ up to fifty people.
Conradh na Gaeilge established Oireachtas na Gaeilge in May 1897 and the Oireachtas is both the largest and oldest festival in Ireland. The festival has grown considerably over the years and it is a great achievement for the people of Derry that Oireachtas na Gaeilge is coming to the city in 2006. This is the second time that the Oireachtas has been in the Six Counties having been in Belfast in 1997.

As part of community building for the Irish speaking community, the Cultúrlann will act as a centre of activity for the city. For years, the strategy which Derry Gaeilgeoirí followed was to stick to the founding principles of Conradh na Gaeilge more than 100 years ago. Life, however, has changed and there is now a pressing need for a strategy that keeps to the founding principles but which also takes on board the current environment. Such a strategy should also use the facilities which are available today but which were not available to preceding generations.

While there is hope in the growth of Irish language education it is also clear that simply sending a child to a gaelscoil is not sufficient Many children coming through the meánscoil do not regard themselves as language activists or indeed as part of the Irish language community in the city. The time has come for us to find a way of creating activists who will take our project on to another level.

I asked Risteard Mac Gabhann, President of Oireachtas 2006, about the changes which he has observed in over fifty years of activism in Derry. He remarked that the word which summed up Irish in those days was 'back-streetism' but that he feels that label has gone and Irish is now on the main street. During the past twenty years, we have made great progress. This ensures that the next generation of language activists will inherit something but more is required than beautiful valuable buildings. We need an intellectual heritage that will guide the revival strategy and language planning.

The gaelscoileanna are probable the greatest sign of hope and there are around 600 children going through that system at present. One question remains, however: is creating young Gaeilgeoirí sufficient? In my view, it is not. We need to create young Gaeilgeoirí who will put the revival on a new level for the coming generation. How will we do that? Some of the city's Irish language groups are currently debating that question.

Since the signing of the Good Friday Agreement and with the establishment of Foras an Gaeilge, and the signing of the Council of Europe Charter, we are gradually leaving the political questions around the language behind us. We have not carried out any exact research into what influenced the progress of the last thirty years. If there is any connection between progress and the struggle against the British or 'the troubles', during the same period, then there is a danger that as the influence of the troubles passes that the same thing will happen in the north as happened in the south in the twenties. I am firmly convinced that the troubles had an influence on language development in the north and that there is a real need to put down deep roots if the progress made is not to stall. I asked a person working with the Irish language in Derry, someone who has no links with the Republican Movement, about the things that inspired him. This is what he said:

There is a commonly held position that the troubles played an influence on the growth of Irish in the city since they inspired Irish people to carve out their own future. People learned Irish as a way of reclaiming their own history and to achieve equality for themselves; an equality not acknowledged by the British nor anyone else, but through their own identity... proof, if you like, that they own this island and that they own this language and all its parts. Those who learned the language during the troubles were returning to their heritage and living as people who were not British, but Irish.

What this means is that today we must create an economic base for the Irish language. We must provide a wide spectrum of jobs; not only in schools but in development of services and setting up companies and giving people the option of living their whole lives through the medium of Irish. In the north, we must put the question of Irish on the programme for government and demand a Language Act that will give proper legal recognition to Irish.

Within the next few years there will be a wonderful outstanding building, designed by John Twomey from Dublin, as a landmark in the centre of Derry and in it Irish will be progressing as a natural part of the lives of the people there. Young Gaeilgeoirí will be sailing a Galway hooker, The Lady Mór, on the Foyle while on the streets of Derry, locals and visitors alike will experience an Irish language ambience in the fourth largest city in Ireland.

An Droichead - The Bridge: South Belfast

Pilib Ó Ruanaí

Background and history

An Droichead is an Irish Language organisation in South Belfast near to the city centre. We have a two acre site on the outskirts of the Lower Ormeau. We mainly serve the people of the Short Strand, a small nationalist area in East Belfast, the Markets area and the Ormeau Road in the south of the city.

There is an Irish medium primary school in our new building as well as an Irish medium pre-school, an after-school club and a youth club. We have at least twenty people employed in all the projects including the school whether in full-time and part-time employment. I believe we are one of the main employers in the area. We have a comprehensive programme of events for the adults and the youth of the area: Irish classes, singing classes, a youth club, set dancing, céilithe, concerts and the like.

Our aim when we began was to nurture an Irish community and it seems that we are gradually achieving our original aim. Our vision for the area has not been completed yet but it is unbelievable the progress which has been made in the last fourteen years.

There are approximately one hundred pupils attending the school and there are currently fifty children in the pre-school. As well as that thirty teenagers attend the youth club every week. Those young people are the foundations of the An Droichead initiative. They are all different kinds of people but they all speak Irish and without our work they would not be Irish speakers.

The beginning of the journey
This is only a personal account of the growth of the group and the work that we have done. It is not a comprehensive account but a one-sided glimpse. Personally, it all began for me in 1989. We had the intention of sending our first born to a gaelscoil. At that time there was only one gaelscoil in Belfast

- Bunscoil Phobail Feirste in Andersonstown - and another one was being set up - Gaelscoil na bhFál on the Falls Road. There were no gaelscoileanna in our area. There was a naíscoil in the Short Strand which was set up in 1981 but at that time in 1989, it was in a poor state. There were only a few infants, there was no staff and the naíscoil was in a run down community centre because the British Government withdrew funding on the basis that the naíscoil was connected to the republican movement.

Swimming against the tide
We would clean the naíscoil on a Friday and on our return on Monday the room would be wrecked by a few thugs from the area. It was heartbreaking and we soon realised that it would not be worth our while carrying on in this way. We spent most of our time raising money and cleaning up the damage that was made. We withdrew from the building and from that area and we amalgamated with the naíscoil in the Markets area.

The Markets Naíscoil
It is only a mile between the Markets and the Short Strand but as is known throughout Ireland another parish is another world entirely. We knew that it would be more difficult to recruit children if parents had to travel out of the area. At the same time if the last naíscoil was in a poor state this one was worse. There was only one committee member doing all the work and the naíscoil had no money. The naíscoil was located in a City Council community centre. There was a snooker table in the middle of the room; the children were forbidden to play with sand and water in case they damaged the floor and there was a rule in place that the curtains were to remain closed at all times during the naíscoil hours in case loyalists found out that a naíscoil - which they thought of as a training camp - was being run inside. It was ridiculous but we had no choice, we had to live with it. We stayed there for two years.

Building a bridge
At some point during this time the main agents came together and we set up a new committee with a new name – An Droichead. The Lagan Bridge was a physical link between the communities and metaphorically speaking we were building a bridge, in a way, to reclaim the Irish language. Instead of thinking parochially about the language we began to contemplate strategically on how to promote Irish in south-east Belfast. We did not fully

understand it at the time but we knew we had to plan and view this initiative in another way.

After two years, in 1993, we were invited by a community group in Lower Ormeau, half a mile away, to be accommodated in their building. I was working for the group at the time as a play worker. The committee was sympathetic to our plight and I knew they would allow me to develop the naíscoil and we would have more independence at least. But again it was a step in the dark: we were moving away from where we began. The committee had to impress on parents that it was to our advantage to move again. It was not easy and we lost children because of the move as one would expect.

At this period, in the early nineties, the troubles were fairly contentious at times and the main road between the Short Strand and the City Centre was often blocked by the RUC. It would take up to an hour and a half to travel to school when normally it took fifteen minutes to get there. You wonder today that people were happy enough to put up with nonsense like this, but they suffered the stress because they thought it was worth it because their children had Irish. It is a small insight into the diligence and the determination of the early pioneers who stood shoulder to shoulder with us in the early days.

A new site
The situation improved when we moved the naíscoil in with the community group; the committee were generous and they gave me freedom to develop the school even though they were my employers. Within a year we had found our present site: a UTV (television company) car park which was used for their BMWs and Mercs. I remember well the first time that I had a meeting with the powers that be in UTV. They were doubtful but we gradually won them over and we got to know each other. They had no intention of selling the land. They did say they would think about it and review their own needs. They added that we would get first refusal if they decided to sell the land.

Fortunately, they kept their word. Six months after my meeting with them they informed us that they were happy to sell the land for £80,000. All we had in the bank was £3,000 but we saw that this was not only a great opportunity but also a good deal. Four of us were happy to get a bank loan together and to make a long story short, after changing banks, we succeeded in getting the required funding.

Soon after this, Ireland experienced the first ceasefire in the troubles. The value of land and houses increased two or threefold, especially in south Belfast, within one year. The land was left idle for three years until we were able to develop it.

In 1995 we secured old mobile huts that belonged to the parish which we fixed up entirely by voluntary workers and we eventually had our own premises again.The naíscoil continued to grow and the nearest gaelscoil could not guarantee places for the children that began in our naíscoil. Therefore, our committee decided to set up a gaelscoil the following year 1996.

The years of 1994 and 1997 saw the biggest growth period in Irish medium education in the north. Six gaelscoileanna were founded: Strabane and Coalisland in Co. Tyrone, Castlewellan in Co. Down, Armagh, Dunloy in Co. Antrim, Ballymurphy, Belfast and another in North Belfast.

A little money was available from the organisation Gaeloiliúint and from a great friend from America, Ray Quinn – who donated up to a million dollars of his own money for the Irish medium cause.

We were conservative because we only had a small community – we knew we would have difficulty in securing funds to employ a teacher and an assistant. We decided at the start to seek Department of Education recognition as a school linked to a school which was already recognised but the Department refused us. We focused on setting up a school with ten children in September 1996 without recognition and without any state funding.

Many people can identify with the struggle that we had trying to run the school without a penny because many's a Gael who did the same before us. But we gradually started to progress in comparison with our counterparts because we secured European Funding which took a lot of pressure off us and allowed us to dedicate our efforts to improving the quality of education.

The school will be ten years old next year and it is going from strength to strength. We now have plans to build a new school building.

The current situation

Lessons
Woody Allen has a proverb which says that presentation is ninety percent of life. I agree totally with him: be there and there is a chance that something will happen.

It is difficult now to think of how much we have learned since we began on this journey; we were so naïve and stupid that every day taught us another lesson. There were four or five on the committee at one time who were all united in their aims – that our children would have Irish. These same people were willing to take responsibility when we employed someone or when we were in arrears with the bank.

As it happens, we did have staff relations problems which were quite bad when some staff and parents opposed the committee. As there were many more people happy to follow the committee's lead we were able to rise above the situation. Those staff members had to be let go and some parents went too but that is the best way because when enough is said and done, it is best to move forward and to part company with people if necessary.

But we learned that we cannot please everyone: the manager has a role and the employee has a role but the various responsibilities of each one need to be clear. When recruiting new staff the new employee should be appointed carefully. There is no real mystery if you keep to the accepted personnel guidelines: job description, a probation period, regular direction etc. But surprisingly even today there are so many organisations in this sector that do not follow those basic guidelines.

From the beginning we were willing as a committee to accept advice from advisors that had experience. We were not afraid to imitate the examples of other groups. In Belfast, at the end of the nineties there were the beginnings of new community structures – forums and various partnerships and we made sure we had places on as many of these bodies as possible. There we received the information and the know-how about funding opportunities. We built up a network of contacts. Most of the people that we met had little or no Irish but it was unbelievable the large amount of good will there exists towards the Irish language.

We appointed advisors as we needed them – a solicitor, a business advisor and an architect. We really could not have done the work without their help. We appointed Seán Mac Goill as an architect when advised by another advisor and he has been our backbone ever since. Seán and then his son Ciarán (after Seán retired) gave us information and technical advice which would lead us to secure substantial grants.

No one has *all* the answers but it is better to be able to raise the appropriate questions and to find someone with some answers.

Dealing with people
It makes sense and it is so obvious that it should not have to be mentioned but this account would be lacking if I did not include the obvious. We are dealing with people. The secretary on the phone, the cleaner in the office, the doorman as well as the 'big shots'; if you deal with them as you would like to be treated – with respect and manners, sooner or later you will see the fruits of your relations with people.

The future

Challenges ahead
We crazy people who began this project have been on a wonderful journey. The project is a company now and we must use the same skills that businesses have – planning, financial planning, staff recruitment, staff management, dealing with all the shareholders - parents, staff, funders, statutory bodies etc. We have new challenges, we have new committee members with the necessary skills to undertake this company and its challenges. We are not under as much pressure as we were – or we know that we have enough money at the end of the month to pay the staff. But we have

more responsibilities as committee members, such as employment legislation, insurance demands and much more.

Monetary sources drying up
Like every other company we keep a keen eye on costs especially as we come to the end of the grants era. The European Union has announced that the special status that Ireland and Britain had will soon end because of European enlargement. The competition in the voluntary sector will make life more and more difficult. From now on we must seek other funding sources. There are activists in the sector looking to the United States, for example, where the voluntary sector gain most of its money from the private sector. The aims of large funders are not the same as the aspirations of charitable associations. We will need to acquire new skills from the business world; there is a possibility that there will be a crossover between business and the voluntary sector. The emphasis is on social economy now – non-profit making groups (Not for Profit) who provide public services such as childcare, meals for pensioners, security etc.and whatever profit is made goes back to the organisation. More of this will happen in the future especially, whilst the authorities will cut back on the services which they offer.

Objectives
There is a three year plan in place that outlines the objectives for An Droichead:

> Increase the number of pupils.
> Consolidate the school and pre school.
> Improve the services that we provide.
> Set up a youth club and develop it.
> Promote our Irish language work in the community.

These objectives are all linked in some way. We must go out and promote our school with parents since the number of children at school going age in Northern Ireland is low.

Parents must be convinced that there is an added value in Irish medium education: at the end of their education their children will be fluent Irish speakers and therefore new doors will open for them. If we succeed in this we will get a permanent building for the school and our pre-school will have a status which will add to the services within the initiative.

We realise that Irish medium education is for a minority and that we should inspire the English medium primary schools and the post- primaries also. Some other community groups in the area have bilingual policies and there are many Irish placenames signs in the area. Our aim is to ensure that Irish be more visible here than it is presently.

The centre is not big enough now for all the daily events. We have drawn up plans with the architect to extend the centre for the after-school services and to build a conference room. Some of the money is still to be raised but a planning application will be submitted shortly. We hope that the work will be finished within a year, with God's help.

In summary
Vision and entrepreneurship are the two things which brought us to where we are today. Now An Droichead has the opportunity to leave its mark on Irish in Belfast and the whole country.

At this point it can be said that 200 children were educated here as well as a few thousand adults. Some young people are working with us now who started here as pre-school children. Time will tell what input they will have on Irish in the future. We have taken the first step to build a community: the youth have Irish, they did not learn under duress - they got the chance to learn it naturally. The old stalwarts must listen to the opinions of the youth and allow them to do their own thing. Unlike us they do not have Irish as a cause - for them it is a means of communication. They will fall in love, they will fall out, they will quarrel, they will create a work of art - just as their colleagues did. But as long as they have a space for Irish in their lives, it can be said that we created an Irish language community.

The youth of today have more talents and are cleverer that we were; they can build on the prototype that we have created, recreate it and renew it. I hope that they enjoy it as much as we did when we laid the foundations.

Irish in Strabane

Seán Ó Dáimhín

Background and history

Strabane is situated on the edge of West Tyrone and borders Donegal at the town of Lifford. The town, with a population of around 13,500 is 93.3% catholic. There are 38,000 (or around 12,000 households) in the wider area which comes under the responsibility of Strabane District Council and which includes the towns of Sion Mills, Newtownstewart, Castlederg and the rural areas around them.

The river Mourne flows through the town dividing it in two, linking with the Finn and the Foyle at the edge of town on the Lifford border. Strabane is a town which suffered much due to having a nationalist majority and being left on the wrong side of the border under British and Unionist rule when the Irish Free State was established. It suffered economically, politically, culturally and socially and the traces of that can still be felt today. There were always difficulties with unemployment and the biggest and most important factory in the town, Adria, is currently laying off workers. Despite these difficulties the community spirit is very strong. Since the mid-nineteen eighties there has been a mini-revolution in language, culture and sport in the town.

At the beginning of the last century in 1901 Gaelic culture underwent a period of growth in Strabane and it was not long until Strabane was in the vanguard of the cultural revolution of Conradh na Gaeilge and the GAA (Gaelic Athletic Association). Irish classes began in the town and local area organised by Brian O'Keeney and someone by the surname of Mac Giolla Dé; Fr. J. McElhatton, and Mícheál Ó Nualláin, the father of the famous author Brian Ó Nualláin (Flann O'Brien, Myles na gCopaleen). Mícheál Ó Nualláin was first Chairperson of the Tyrone County Board of the GAA in 1904. In 1902 Strabane was given a specific mention in an article in the journal *An Claidheamh Soluis* entitled A Northern Centre of Gaelic Work. In June 1903 a Feis Mhór was organised in Strabane which was billed as the 'most important Gaelic meeting in the northwest' at the time. And the area has its own Gaelic heroes: George Sigerson (after whom the Sigerson Cup in Gaelic football is named); Flann O'Brien who wrote An Béal Bocht and his brother Ciarán Ó Nualláin who was once editor of the Irish language newspaper Inniu.

Going through back issues of the past hundred years of the Strabane Chronicle one can see both individuals and organisations working at different times to keep the language and the Gaelic culture alive and developing. Two names pop up again and again: Gearóid Mac an Chrosáin, who died in 1989, and Gearalt Ó Dochartaigh who died in 2003. It would be clear to anyone who spoke to Gearalt Ó Dochartaigh for even five minutes that he was inspired by the vision of Pearse. He had spent more than fifty years organising Irish classes in the town. He was active in Conradh na Gaeilge, Comhaltas Uladh, and the GAA, He had spent time in prison and he used to write to republican prisoners and visit us. He was a morale boost to spend time with and his interest in the Irish language never waned.

Why do I mention these two? There were others also who did good work and then moved on. But I do not think anyone can mention any form of revival in this town without mentioning these two men and remembering the huge influence they had on us all. It is no wonder that the name of Gearóid is today remembered in the local Craobh of Conradh na Gaeilge (Craobh Ghearóid Mhic Chrosáin) and that Gearalt's name is to be found in the name of the local gaelscoil. I also mention them for other reasons. At the beginning of the eighties Gaelic culture was at a low ebb in Strabane. Apart from a few classes and the occasional event there was nothing else happening, although Gearóid and Gearalt were both involved in these activities. I attended a few classes in 1982 when I was 18 years old. However it looked then as if they were fighting a lost cause despite all their life's work and that there would be very little to show for all their efforts.

Then in the ten years between 1987 and 1997 a language revolution began in the town which has not ended yet, a mini-revolution which impacts on education, social, cultural and political life.

At the beginning a group of young people and students who had learned Irish at school and university came together. They were full of energy and fresh ideas. They joined Conradh na Gaeilge and the older generation, the middle aged and the youth came together. The classes were re-organised with new teaching methods. Irish language street signs were erected in Strabane. There were regular articles in the papers. Competitions were organised for the young people. There were trips to Tigh Mhaggie Mhánuis (RIP) in Gort an Choirce in the Donegal Gaeltacht. The town had a nationalist population and it was not long until these events were attracting more and more people. The image of the Craobh was different from the usual image of a Craobh of Conradh na Gaeilge. Another boost came with the renewed interest in GAA in the town from 1986 when Tyrone reached the All-Ireland final and when the Sigerson GAA Club was re-established and re-organised in the area.

Another huge step in the cultural revolution was taken in September 2004 when Naíscoil an tSratha Bháin opened under the patronage of Conradh na Gaeilge. This was the first all-Irish pre-school in Tyrone and it was officially opened by Proinsias Mac Aonghusa. Great changes followed the opening. Young parents were now part of the language revolution and a new voice was added to that of the old activists, students and other individuals who had always been interested in the language. Many of these parents did not speak Irish but they had other skills that could be used to the benefit of the cause.

I had no connection with any of this work. At the time I was in Long Kesh, but it was a great source of pride to the Strabane prisoners that Strabane was awakening to the language. Máirtín Ó Maolmhuaidh, a comrade of mine from Strabane, was in charge of the Culture Department in Long Kesh and his family were involved in the language revival outside. He kept us abreast of all that was happening. Some of us were coming to the end of our sentences and were eager to be out to take part in the work. Many prisoners took an interest in language revival as we gained an awareness of how important it is to the national identity.

I was brought up with English, which should not be surprising. I do not know anyone in Strabane the same age as myself who was brought up with Irish. I do not know anyone the same age as myself who ever spoke a word of Irish when they were young. I did not even know that Irish existed until I went into Primary 7 at the Primary school and a teacher gave us a few lessons even though it was not on the curriculum. I was lucky to take Irish as a subject at the secondary school in St. Colmán's where less that two out of every seven were given the opportunity to learn Irish. However I did not really learn Irish at school. It was only another school subject, that is how we looked at it. Whatever knowledge I have of Irish and whatever interest I have in it came much later during my time in Long Kesh. Many prisoners tell the same story. We used to have Irish classes all the time and then in the nineties we set up Gaeltacht na Fuiseoige in Long Kesh where only Irish was allowed to be spoken.

I was released in December 1995. I was given a class to teach in January. I joined Conradh na Gaeilge and was made Rúnaí of the local Craobh. At that time there were classes for all ages in the Melvin Hall in Strabane. Other classes were set up in other centres in the town and in Sion Mills. There were parents, students, ex-prisoners, pre-school workers, Gearalt Ó Dochartaigh and other people working day and night promoting Irish in Strabane. Voluntarily.

Then, a few parents began talking about Irish language schooling. Some of them felt that there was little point in sending their children to an Irish pre-school if they were not going on to an Irish language primary school. The question was debated at naíscoil meetings but even more so in houses and in conversations between friends. Various different opinions came to the fore. Some felt that the town was not ready for a bunscoil Gaeilge yet. They were worried that damage would be done to the language if the school opened prematurely and failed. There were others whose children were attending the naíscoil and felt they would not have a second chance.

A resolution to the problem came from outside. The naíscoil organised a public meeting in May 1997 to discuss Irish language schooling. At the time we were thinking of organising a bus to take the children to Bunscoil Cholm Cille, fourteen miles away in Derry. Cathal Ó Donnghaile from the organisation Gaeloiliúint attended the meeting along with parents, members of Conradh na Gaeilge, the committee and workers from the naíscoil etc. Different views were expressed and while it was clear that they all had an interest in Irish they all had different opinions regarding it. Then Cathal spoke and explained the situation. He explained to us that , in his opinion, it was the right time to set up a gaelscoil in Strabane. We looked at each other. He had an answer for every question and after an hour of discussion it was agreed to open a gaelscoil in Strabane the following September. However many different individuals and groups came into that meeting, we left as a single group, with a single vision, to open a gaelscoil in our own district.

I do not want to write the history of the gaelscoil here but it is worth mentioning a few things that might give encouragement to other areas that are considering opening a gaelscoil.

When we began we did not have a building, nor even a room nor money, teachers, books or any other facility. We had no school uniforms, nor even a name for our school or any recognition from the community. On the first day we opened with four children. People would ask 'Are there no professional people on your committee?' Ordinary people and ordinary parents set up the school. If we had waited on the professionals, the school would never have opened. The people of the town supported the vision, they supported the fundraising draws and every other scheme we organised. And they sent their children to the school. There are around 150 children attending the naíscoil and gaelscoil at present.

In 1986, when Tyrone played Kerry in the All Ireland Final, it would have been nigh on impossible for the likes of Ráidió na Gaeltachta or RTÉ 1 to have found a single young person in the town capable of giving an interview through Irish. In September 2005 when Tyrone brought the Sam Maguire Cup home for the second time, Ráidió na Gaeltachta and TG4 were in Strabane interviewing many children and families who speak Irish. Success follows success.

The current situation

Something else happened at the meeting of May 1997. An organisation known as Gaelphobal was established, a name suggested by Cathal Ó Donnghaile as he was leaving the meeting. Gaelphobal had two roles at the beginning: to set up a gaelscoil and to co-ordinate the financial arrangement between the gaelscoil, the naíscoil and Conradh na Gacilge. Gradually, however, Gaelphobal's role changed. It began as an umbrella group for all three committees (Coiste na Gaelscoile, Coiste na Naíscoile and Craobh Ghearóid Mhic an Chrosáin of Conradh na Gaeilge). Between 1997 and 2004, to be honest, all the attention was on establishing and giving a secure footing to schooling through Irish in this area. None of the three committees had either the time or resources for any other major development. We employed a Development Officer for an eighteen month period with assistance from European funding. We found land for the two schools and they were built. We spent a lot of time increasing the number of children attending the schools. We brought the two schools into the everyday conversation of the local people. We won the prize for Best New Entry in Glór na nGael. We employed a part time youth officer and we won the Youth Prize in Glór na nGael. We gathered money annually and we are still collecting. And the gaelscoil was given state recognition in the year 2000.

I think one of the strongest things in Strabane is the forging of links between the Irish language groups through the umbrella group Gaelphobal. We have our own problems, of course, disputes between committees, between people; something that I now know is unavoidable when a small group of people is highly active, although of course the disputes should be recognised and resolved as far as is possible. I also know, however, that there are other areas of the country where the local Conradh has not a clue about their local gaelscoil and where there is little co-operation between them. Until 2004 Gaelphobal was functioning as an umbrella group for the three committees already mentioned. Each committee sent two representatives to meetings of Gaelphobal but to be frank the work began to fall off. So much work had been put into setting up the school and into running classes and attending meetings that some of us were beginning to lose energy. We did not have anyone employed to carry out the work. Our application to Foras na Gaeilge failed in 2002 and we did not enter the Glór na nGael competition. We needed new blood, or fresh ideas.

In the autumn of 2004 we received a copy of Scéim Phobail Fhoras na Gaeilge. There was reference in it to a school community. There was reference to partnership. These two themes stood out for us. We were lucky that all of us understood the need for a fresh development. At the beginning we felt that the partnership that existed between the committees through Gaelphobal was enough but gradually we came to a new concept. We decided on a new approach. We would create a proper partnership between ourselves and Foras na Gaeilge on one hand and we would also have to create partnerships with new organisations in west Tyrone. We would need a worker to take on the additional work but the term Development Worker did not suit us as it was not active enough for us. We agreed on the term Irish Language Community Organiser. We would put up half of the funding to cover the costs of the job and the office. Rather than value in kind we were putting up hard cash that we would collect annually and this was the partnership we created with Foras na Gaeilge who put up the remainder of the funding.

The second partnership we created was to speak to people in Gortin and Castlederg. There is a naíscoil and gaelscoil in Gortin, thirteen miles from Strabane and there are classes for all ages in Castlederg twelve miles from Strabane. The people of Castlederg would like to set up a naíscoil as soon as possible. Two new committees and two new districts joined Gaelphobal at the end of 2004. We meet every month and there is now fresh energy and new ideas coming forward as well as skills and experience from our friends in Castlederg and Gortin.

An Ógras youth club was established in Strabane in 2005. The Club is located in Fountain Street Community Centre, a centre equipped with the best of resources: a computer room, a sports hall, an art room, an astroturf park, an office and kitchen. We prefer using the community's own facilities instead of developing a separate Irish language centre because we have far more influence on the community when we are using the same facilities as them. For example some of them are now putting up notices in the two languages about general activities. This would not happen if we were cooped up in the gaelscoil or some other centre. It is also an advantage that we aren't liable for huge running costs and that gives us more time to spend on developing Irish.

A branch of Comhluadar for families has also been established. Comhluadar staged a huge event in Gortin during the weekend of February 18th 2006 with the start of Gaelchónaí na Speiríní. Forty people were set to take part: families, parents learning Irish, children attending the gaelscoil, all staying in Gortin Accommodation Centre, and spending the whole weekend through the medium of Irish. The last native speaker of Irish in Tyrone lived in Gortin and it was fitting that it was there that the first mini-Ghaeltacht was established even if it were only to last for a weekend. We would like to repeat this pilot program a couple of times each year, helping parents to break from the language habit of speaking English with their children and demonstrating to them that it is possible to exist without speaking English.

The Diploma course in Irish from Ollscoil na hÉireann, Gaillimh has begun in Strabane and there are plenty of other courses from the Northwest Institute for Further and Higher Education. We publish a newsletter as often as possible and the local paper has bilingual and Irish language articles every week. Strabane District Council has just adopted a Language Diversity Policy in which commitments have been made to Irish and to services through Irish. Representatives of Gaelphobal are on the monitoring committee for that policy. Strabane is now recognised as an area where Irish is growing and other groups are now seeking our opinions. For example Pobal held a meeting in the area regarding the drafting of a Language Act for the Six Counties. There is a revival of the revival, if you see what I mean.

The future

Where would we like to be in ten years time? Firstly Irish should be strengthened in the educational system in the Six Counties and it is my belief that this factor is more important than anything else at this time. Parents are often in touch with me asking Irish language groups in Strabane to organise Irish classes for their children because the language is not available in their schools. There is a general opinion that the language organisations in the Six Counties are excelling in the promotion of Irish and that notion is being used as an argument to make Irish optional in the education system in the twenty six counties. However I can say this much, as a person who was educated in the Six Counties but who works in the Public Service in the twenty six Counties at present, there is no basis to that argument. When I take a beginners' class for adults in Strabane it would break your heart to see the number of people who have never even heard the word 'tá' in their lives. It takes three or four years to bring a person in the north to a level of conversational Irish. In the twenty six counties when someone starts a bunrang and says they have 'no Irish' it takes only about eight weeks until they have conversational Irish. That is the big difference between 'the great silence' in the north and having the basic language skills in the twenty six counties.

The second objective I would like to see achieved is the development of the three Irish language communities of Strabane, Castlederg and Gortin as part of the wider community round us. There is always the danger, because many people in the community have absolutely no Irish, that we will always be separate, in a life of our own cut off from other community developments. We do not want that. And that is the real challenge, a challenge that is bigger and greater in the Six Counties.

Immigrants and the Irish language - 2005 and onwards

Ariel Killick

Background and history

Massive change took place in Ireland between 1996 and 2005 when, for the first time, more people were coming into Ireland looking for work and a better life than were leaving for America, England and further abroad in search of the same. The implications of these changes for the Irish language had not gone entirely unnoticed, but little happened until immigrants saw that it was as much in their own interest, as for the benefit of the language, that the issue be addressed properly. In February 2005, Alex Hijmans, an Irish-speaking Dutch journalist based in Galway, wrote a sombre and controversially speculative article discussing the potential for future fascists to use the language as a rallying point against immigrants. Alex noted that people rarely called him about articles he penned for the national Irish language weekly, Foinse, but after that article he got three calls: one from Fachtna Ó Drisceoil, an RTÉ journalist who had previously written about the same issue; John Walsh, an eminent lecturer in sociolinguistics in NUI Galway and myself, an Irish-speaking Australian translator and artist living in Ireland. Coincidentally, I happened to be on the train to Galway for a television engagement the day the article was published and so arranged to meet Alex later in the evening to talk about ways of ensuring that what he had forecast in his article would not come to pass.

Immigrants had already been used by people only too ready to ditch Irish, to argue that a traditional aspect of Irish multilingualism should be further demoted in favour of languages newer to Ireland, and comments such as 'We're all Europeans now, we should learn Spanish instead of Irish', or ' More people in Ireland speak Chinese than Irish', and 'Compulsory Irish is racist', were becoming more familiar. We saw what many Irish people did not; engaging immigrants and immigration against Irish in this way set immigrants up to be scapegoated for any future erosion of the language and played directly into the hands of those who could contribute to creating the dire scenario we sought to prevent.

By further bizarre coincidence, I happened to be booked to perform at an event in Galway the following Wednesday with former college housemate and colleague, magician Tony Pratschke. Tony was born in Cork but his father had come to Ireland from Czechoslovakia during World War II and Tony had also converted to Islam later in life. Tony, Alex and I decided to meet that fateful Wednesday to follow up on our meeting on Saturday, and shortly after that, iMeasc was born on 24 April 2005, in the new Irish language centre, Gaelchultúr, in Temple Bar, Dublin, one year to the day after the march through Dublin demanding Stádas for the Irish language in the EU.

At the time of that march in April 2004, the Acting CEO of Conradh na Gaeilge, Aoife Ní Scolaí, had called for a 'carnival atmosphere' for the protest and since I had much experience as a stilt walker, and against a backdrop of the Citizenship Referendum and the debate around immigrants, I decided to take up the call. Over eight foot tall, dressed in an elaborate fire-themed costume with 'Inimirceoirí ar son Gaeilge/Immigrants for Irish' painted on my bare back, a mini media frenzy immediately ensued as six or so photographers sprang around me with two nearly getting into a fight with each other. The resulting image was used often in coverage of the Stádas issue, but with the birth of iMeasc a year later, what had started out on a once relatively carefree street entertainer's back had transformed into something so much more serious that it would end up with me addressing no less than a Joint Oireachtas Committee in the Dáil and a seminar on the Irish language at the Progressive Democrats' National Conference just under two years later. I did not bring my stilts.

The first meeting in April 2005 was attended by six fluent Irish-speaking immigrants: Andreas Vogel from Germany; Michal Boreslav Merchura from the Czech Republic; Chantal Kobel from Switzerland; Colleen Dollard from Washington, Alex and myself. There were also some Irish-born people present, journalist Fachtna Ó Drisceoil, Siobhán Nic Ghaoithín, who was working with Conradh na Gaeilge in Galway teaching Irish to refugees; Pádraig Ó Laighin, a returned emigrant from Canada and head of the Stádas campaign and Anna Heusaff, another interested Irish language journalist of mixed cultural background. After a roundtable discussion, I was elected Chairperson and the name iMeasc was chosen for the group to reflect both the concept of integration and respect, incorporating as it does the various words 'Imeasc, measc, i measc, meas' or 'Integrate, mix, amongst, respect'.

Two further meetings took place at which Alex was elected Vice-chairperson and we drew up a list of aims for the group:

1. To encourage immigrants to learn Irish and to use Irish in order to interact with that part of Irish culture:
   as a means for better integrating themselves, their children and their cultural identity within society;
   and as a means to integrate in Irish society in a healthy, peaceful, sustainable way in the long-term.
2. To disseminate information about Irish amongst immigrants by:
   encouraging Irish language organisations to include immigrants in their work;
   encouraging immigrant organisations to include Irish in their work;
   addressing attempts to utilise immigrants in arguments against Irish or Irish in arguments against immigrants.

and to accomplish these aims through the following actions:
1. Publicising the group and its aims through the media, with politicians, community organisations, and representatives of immigrant groups with the objective of showing that immigrants can achieve high levels of fluency in Irish; that many of them wish to achieve this or at least some fluency in Irish; and that this is a good thing in itself and also in respect of point 2 mentioned above.
2. Acting as positive role models for both immigrants and Irish people with a view to achieving point 1 mentioned above.
3. Achieving representation in the school, gaelscoil and Irish language sectors.

4. Integrating immigrants and immigrants who speak Irish in Irish language education, textbooks and in the Irish language sector/scene generally.

5. Making submissions to state departments, and appropriate bodies and organisations to inform them of our existence and to advance our objectives.

It was not long before aims became action. When an Irish Times editorial questioned the value of the Official Languages Act by stating that most immigrants would choose to speak English, nine of us signed a letter in response disputing the insinuation that English would be the sole language of choice for immigrants, and also highlighting not only the various areas we worked in with Irish but the fact that some of us had studied Irish prior to coming to Ireland. Nuacht TG4 contacted us the day the letter was published, and the interview broadcast that night was to become the first of many.

Events soon after would prove just how timely, and fortunate, the establishment of iMeasc was. When many people were suggesting immigrants were a threat to the Irish language on foot of plans by the Minister for Justice to change the entry requirements in relation to Irish for the Garda Síochána, Alex and I were in place and ready to take up the challenge in the name of iMeasc. We had a series of interviews with both the Irish language and English language media to talk about our fluent Irish-speaking members, how learning Irish had benefited them and how they, in turn, were working in various areas to the benefit of the Irish language and of the Irish people in general. A letter outlining why training in Irish should remain a part of the Garda training course and be made available to all recruits, regardless of cultural background, was drafted and sent to all who were involved in the change process.

We met with a Sergeant in Templemore responsible for designing the new Irish language course, and further media interviews followed. Whilst most went very well, an interview on Newstalk FM was by far the most difficult. A teacher called in saying that I was off the planet whilst 'You don't understand our culture, we hate Irish', was one of the more memorable text comments to come in.

Two other lesser campaigns were also directed through the letters columns of the Irish Times, Daily Ireland and Foinse following letters from readers upset at the changes in recruitment procedures to the Garda. iMeasc stood up for both Irish-speaking immigrants and solidarity with the language and made the point that Irish people needed to speak Irish themselves before demanding interest and support in the language from immigrants. The Irish Examiner published a full-page article on the issue shortly after with two people from iMeasc, highlighting the quote 'It's pretty repugnant when people say immigrants are a threat to Irish – start speaking it yourself.' The opportunity to stress this aspect in the article arose from yet another freak co-incidence, namely that the features editor of the Examiner was a fellow Australian who was sympathetic to my views that the hypocrisy of people who had just enough interest in Irish to use it in arguments against immigrants, or vice versa, but not enough to bother speaking or learning it themselves, needed to be countered.

I was invited to speak at an educational conference being organised by Conradh na Gaeilge later that year and, from a chance meeting through a friend, facilitated the visit of a Basque language activist working with immigrants in her region to speak at the conference. I was also personally invited to become a member of the Coiste Gnó (Business Committee) of Conradh na Gaeilge by its Uachtarán (President) the very morning that Foinse published a piece about iMeasc shortly after its establishment. Joe Higgins, a socialist T.D. who had earned the respect of many due to his stand on issues regarding foreign workers in both Gama and Irish Ferries, later invited Alex and myself to the Dáil for lunch and his support and advice were instrumental in facilitating an address to a Joint Committee of the Oireachtas in conjunction with Conradh na Gaeilge in March 2006.

The current situation

iMeasc also had substantial plans to achieve more than simply drawing attention to ourselves in the media. A list of ten proposals was drawn up and forwarded to the CEOs of Údarás na Gaeltachta and Foras na Gaeilge and meetings were held shortly after. Whilst the change in CEO for Foras na Gaeilge meant that some time passed before we could properly bring the plans forward, highly constructive discussions are ongoing at the time of writing (2005). Our recommendations were as follows:

a That arrangements be made for Irish language outreach work with regard to immigrants through the creation of an Outreach Officer in Irish language organisations to implement the following both regionally and nationally;

b Provision of classes in Irish to any group of refugees and their children being located in Gaeltacht areas, or close to a gaelscoil and contact to be made with any large group of immigrants in a particular area (for example the Brazilian community in Gort in Co Galway) to offer this service;

c Formulation and distribution of three-way phrase books (Irish –English – Chinese etc.) through the various immigrant organisations, launched at intercultural events for particular ethnic groups, introducing them to Irish culture through Irish, English and their own language. This would also provide an opportunity for people interested in Irish to learn about other cultures while also giving an opportunity to people from the ethnic groups to meet Irish speakers. A series of such events could be launched under the theme of An Ghaeilge do Chách (Irish is for Everyone) led by a celebrity such as Seán Óg Ó hAilpín (captain of the successful Cork Hurling team and of Fijian and Irish parentage); or co-ordinated with a website giving profiles of different Irish speaking immigrants. The website could be in Irish, English or other immigrant languages, and could also include information about the language and what is available (books, classes, social events etc, with a link to www.gaeilge.ie.) There could also be a few bilingual games for children, for example one in Ibo/Yoruba and Irish;

d Funding for a short-term research project to put together the stories of Irish-speaking immigrants and how Irish has worked for them, and for a suitable website to spread the word further;

e Formulation of training courses to fully utilise the resource of foreign-trained teachers who have passed the Irish language qualification exam and who could provide courses in Irish through languages other than English (for those whose mother tongue is not English, this having been identified as an extra barrier to learning Irish by one of our German members working in Conamara), and to help immigrants to acquire the language as well as children attending school in the Gaeltacht who have neither Irish nor English (including the children of returned emigrants), or to act as language assistants in Gaelscoileanna/English language schools;

f Ensuring that children in gaelscoileanna are given a range of opportunities to interact with children from different backgrounds and to approach this through, for example, arranging music workshops with musicians from different backgrounds such as Jaba Jaba Djembe from Ghana who speaks some Irish (seas suas, bualadh bos etc.) with the children during their workshops;

g Discussion of the question with the European Network for State Minority Language Bodies at their conference on 11 November 2005;

h Organisation of a seminar to discuss the issue with the main partners in educational provision in Ireland.

The future

Irish language organisations themselves need to include immigrants in their work, and develop an outreach role to forward the aims we laid out at the beginning. The issue also needs to be looked at within immigrant services organisations to ensure that immigrants are made aware of and integrated into the huge growth in Irish language activity over the last few years. I foresee that this growth is set to continue, as, due to net inwards migration, Irish people become more aware of the importance of language in defining cultural identity.

Due to repeated reports of children of immigrant background excelling at Irish in schools, we can reasonably expect some of these children to grow to be leaders and innovators in Irish, much as some of those in iMeasc and higher profile personalities such as Seán Óg Ó hAilpín have done. We need to make space for these people now, work to create a society in which Irish plays an integrating role and move away from a view that sees the language and immigrants as incompatible.

Reflections

iMeasc has no monopoly on our aims or recommendations, and it is my hope that all Irish language and immigrant service organisations will integrate into their own activities some of the aims we formulated for the benefit of Irish and intercultural peace in general in Ireland.

Conclusion

Helen Ó Murchú

Our thanks go to the Chief Executive and the Steering Committee of Glór na nGael for this valuable publication which provides ten case studies from different communities throughout the country, vividly illustrating their efforts to revive, strengthen and retain the Irish language in their respective areas, given in an easily accessible forthright style not given to jargon.

The diversity of these areas adds greatly to the value of the information and the analysis given. Among them are two initiatives in the Gaeltacht, three from Northern Ireland, two from the suburbs of Dublin and a further two in regional towns. They are complemented by a comprehensive account from the Chief Executive of Foras na Gaeilge on language planning as currently viewed by that body as well as a report on immigrants and the Irish language, a subject very much *ad rem* to modern Irish society.

It is useful that each of the contributors is or has been personally active in the effort to make a bilingual society a reality. It is from experience, bitter experience at times, that their insights have been forged. And that is where the true benefit of these differing accounts of activism lie, in a publication that encapsulates forty years of voluntary action for the Irish language, activism that Glór na nGael has inspired. It would be a worthwhile exercise to consider each and every one of these individual studies both in the context of the language planning framework for the future provided by Foras na Gaeilge and from the viewpoint of the activists working on the ground, as well as in the context of the natural organic development in their approach over the years.

In a comprehensive and history-rich article on Paróiste an Chnoic, tracing community development in the region since the 1960s, including the first community initiative Cois Fharraige, Peadar Mac an Iomaire, a former Chairman of Glór na nGael's Steering Committee, reminds us that activism is continually developing, changing, evolving. This is echoed in every case study in this publication, particularly in the contribution on Uíbh Ráthach from Caitlín Bhreathnach and Seán Mac an tSíthigh, the weakest Gaeltacht in the country, surviving in a completely different context to that of Cois Fharraige, arguably the strongest Gaeltacht. People have been working in the cause of the language in Uíbh Ráthach only for some short few years now but the rapid evolution of thinking on development there has currently reached the point where there is on the one hand an understanding of the cold reality that the position of the native language is greatly weakened while on the other hand an action plan is already being implemented which well predates the recommendations of Foras na Gaeilge, though it is largely organised in similar planning terms.

According to these accounts on different Gaeltachtaí, the problems are generally the same for each of them, as are the solutions that they are deploying which encompass both language based initiatives and language focused staff working on language planning pilot schemes. If this approach is late, it is also timely. There was a time when it was the accepted common wisdom that it is possible to separate the state of a language and culture and the state of an economy from each other rather than adopt a cohesive all-inclusive approach. Nonetheless, with regard to language planning, one must raise the question as to whether there exists, or should exist, a qualitative difference between language planning in and for the Gaeltacht and language planning outside of the Gaeltacht. And if such planning evolves and changes organically over time to meet changing needs, is it possible to intervene and to direct that evolution so as to achieve the best possible results. Even the manner in which the rhetoric and the public discourse on language matters change over time is in itself indicative of that evolution, of course.

Reading through the various articles, it is the similarities between the various areas that strike the reader, particularly the practical activities that were chosen to strengthen the language in the community, be that community in the north, in the south, in the east or in the west. It hardly matters which region. Is that lack of differentiation a weakness or a strength? Even more than these similarities, however, it is the pioneering mentality, ambitions and spirit of the activists who initiated the projects that are described in these pages which most impress the reader. In the words of Eoghan Mac Cormaic, GLOR Bhaile Locha Riach, they are people 'who believed'. The terms 'aisling' and vision are used frequently. The realisation of the vision is the most commonly used phrase. They were people who wanted better for their families or for their communities. People who realised something was missing and who aspired to do something about it. The stories recounted here are those of a family, an individual, or a group taking up the linguistic challenge, against the opposing tide of communal and political wisdom with which they were faced.

It is also apparent how spirit leaves its mark by inspiring others in the vicinity, the influence of those who went before leaving their own imprint on later generations. These are factors not easily articulated in the usual concept of what constitutes a rational plan. Each of the contributors to this publication is steeped in the traditions and history of our forebears. The role of the voluntary organisations is also evident. The oldest organisation, Conradh na Gaeilge, is still a source of philosophy (although Gearóid Ó hEára, Derry, reckons that matters philosophic might need tailoring for today's exigencies). The newer specialist service providers, Naíonraí, Gaelscoileanna, Comhluadar, constitute sources of support for the development of language based initiatives.

Interesting issues are raised by the contributors. It is clear that the authors know the dangers that are presented by a lack of successors for the founding group. Energy dissipates, explains Proinsias Ó hAilín in regard to Muintir Chrónáin. Writing about An Droichead, Pilib Ó Ruanaí claims that the youth need to be empowered for the cultural challenges they have yet to face and that the more seasoned activists need to give them space to develop – something that is not always easy. Ariel Killick, an immigrant, goes so far as to say that iMeasc, the project with which she is associated, ought to be a temporary one. She believes that it is up to the long established Irish language organisations to integrate the aims of iMeasc into their own regular work programmes. Self-destruction – that is an approach not often seen in the voluntary sector. Eoghan Mac Cormaic poses a further difficult question with regard to cohesion and the desired co-operation. Is it possible to use more effectively the type of independence that comes to the fore when specialist working groups emerge in order to achieve a particular element from a list of aims, each participant group having their own separate vision.

In spite of the constant emphasis in the articles on the importance of Irish medium education and the good results emanating from it, it is clear to Gearóid Ó hEára in his account from Derry that it is not enough to develop such Irish medium education if the circle is not completed; in other words, if those children attending do not in turn become activists in the footsteps of their predecessors. Brian Mac Aongusa sees a further role for these children in his report on south Dublin since the 1940s – firstly the creation of networks of former pupils across a range of professions and secondly the firm hope that, as parents, these former pupils will, in turn, send their children to gaelscoileanna. However, do such loose networks of former gaelscoil pupils constitute a language community?

Although it is the kernel of each article that a cultural problem or vacuum was identified, the approach to finding a solution was not the same in every case. In Carlow, Bríde de Róiste explains, the arts inspired the festival, Éigse Cheatharlach, as a means of initially raising the profile of the language since the group of activists were starting from a very low base. In Clondalkin, Dublin, although the founding aim of Muintir Chrónáin was to ensure an Irish medium bunscoil (primary school), it was decided to build broad-based community support first, particularly through aspects of culture, in order to assuage any doubts over lack of ability in the language as a negative factor among possible supporters. However, in the majority of examples in this publication, Irish medium education was indeed the prime inspiration and the premier aim. Nevertheless, other contextual aspects were quickly identified: that knowledge and ability in a language are not enough unless it is interwoven with a rich and strong underlying cultural base; that the context of the school alone does not suffice but that provision of appropriate events for youth and for job opportunities at a later stage are crucial; that there is also a need to expand as far as possible into neighbouring geographic areas to widen the physical context. If sustainability is sought, there must be comprehensive linguistic provision for all aspects of life rather than mere tokenism. Ability without ensuing appropriate contexts of use has long bedevilled language planning in Ireland. To cultural motivation must be added instrumental and economic motivation. In addition, comprehensive analysis must be the norm from the start as well as continual assessment as opposed to ad hoc unconnected actions. Therein lie the lessons for all serious readers of this publication.

The various projects which are recounted here are all at different stages of development but comprehension of these progressive lessons can be found in all of them. It is apparent from Seán Ó Dáimhin's account of Strabane that it is catching up with An Droichead and that an Droichead in turn is catching up with Derry. It is interesting to compare Strabane and Loughrea as two fairly new projects. Loughrea is young compared to Carlow but is broadening out from the town already into neighbouring territory, just as Derry has done.

In the official research on public opinion carried out in the 1970s, (CLAR – Committee on Language Attitudes Research), it is recognised that in language matters there are three variables which are interdependent and interactive: attitude, ability and use. In general, for the majority of people, the more they use a language the more their ability increases; ability and usage help to create a positive disposition; similarly positive attitudes nurture the disposition to increase ability and usage. Without a positive attitude, it is not easy to operate. A person operates as part of a community and not in a vacuum. Both subjective and objective influences operate on each person as an individual, and as part of a community, in building personal identity. There are few people who would wish to be identified with or be part of some thing, or some community, which is associated with failure, difficulties, scorn or abuse. An individual can hardly be blamed for seeking that which produces satisfyingly good results, that which appears to attract public good will. This is very clear in the effect of Éigse in Carlow. It stirred hope in the community; self-respect was re-awakened in the community. Likewise in Uíbh Ráthach, where the revival began in the 1990s with Éigse na Brídeoige and in Strabane where efforts have achieved unexpected results, or in any one of the examples in this publication. The gospel, the good news, is needed and sought by individuals and by communities.

But the Irish language is still a hidden resource. It is of little surprise that Bríde de Róiste claims that it was through the back door that the language slipped through Éigse; that Risteard Mac Gabhann reports that the Irish language has now moved from the back street and onto the main street; or that Caitlín Bhreathnach and Seán Mac an tSíthigh claim that the language has moved from the periphery in Uíbh Ráthach to the centre stage. It is clear in every case, as explained by Caitlín and Seán, that communities are celebrating their own identity again; that it is finding again self-confirmation and community cohesion.

Valuable as these results are, are they sufficient as criteria to assert that these different language projects are in fact succeeding or indeed what might be the appropriate criteria for success? The contributors have shown remarkable honesty. Despite the evidence that they have achieved many of their fundamental targets, particularly in terms of the numbers of children attending Irish medium education, the establishment of institutions or the organisation of community events, these contributors do not shy away from the difficulties or from the challenges. Among these they list: people in every community who refuse to take part; the particular case of people who are willing to help but who do not have Irish and who do not possess the disposition to learn; that at times a bilingual approach has to be taken; the lack of cooperation among Irish language organisations; the apparent end to voluntary action in today's busy world and the subsequent need to employ people dedicated to the language.

It is important also to mention politics - local, regional and national. It is difficult for the people of Uíbh Ráthach, for example, to differentiate between the support from Foras na Gaeilge, Údarás na Gaeltachta and the Department of Community, Rural and Gaeltachta Affairs when their area covers districts both within and outside the Gaeltacht. Caitlín Bhreathnach and Seán Mac an tSíthigh advise that plans put before official funders should not be overly complicated. It is possible that the fundamental problem is, however, that cohesive planning is needed to bring an end to parallelism. Peadar Mac an Iomaire has nothing but praise for the continuing support of the Minister for the Gaeltacht, although he reminds us also of the political reasons which led to the movement Cearta Sibhialta na Gaeltachta (Civil Rights for the Gaeltacht) being necessary. Likewise, Carlow has strong praise for the Department of Education. In the case of Derry and Loughrea, matters of party politics were the cause of difficulties due to the involvement of members of Sinn Féin in the projects. In any relatively small community, questions of this nature will be raised, especially if things are succeeding and particularly in the context of the history of the past thirty years in this country. They are fundamentally questions of power and the sharing of power. The only way they can be answered is with honesty from the start and acceptance of the reality that the language belongs to everyone. It is worth remembering that, in matters linguistic, the relationship between the citizen and the state is not the same north and south in Ireland, at least not yet. Initiatives providing cultural support for the UVF (Ulster Volunteer Force) are not seen in the south. By and large, it must be accepted that the business of language conservation is in itself a political act. Language matters and political matters cannot be separated at community level, unlike at individual level. The public good, the state, citizens of the state, members of the nation, civil society, policies that relate to these at all levels – these are all intrinsically related yet differentially interpreted.

It appears from the various accounts given in this publication that the main planning problem lies not so much in the lack of plans as in the lack of professional planners. But formal public planning is a reasonably new concept. Not that planning was not being applied but rather that it had not yet reached the status of a discipline in its own right. As with any multi-disciplinary or inter-disciplinary activity, the concept of language planning is relatively new and is still evolving. There is a difference between planning for the economy, for example, or for some aspect of the economy such as infrastructure or roads, and planning for that which constitutes a human dynamic and social inter-activity. In addition, it is less problematic to set about language planning in terms of corpus planning for dictionaries and specific terminology, or acquisition planning through education, or planning for the use and extension of use of a language by the public through legislation. Up a point, it is easier to carry out such objective planning for a language separate from its speech community (reification of language, from the Latin res which means a thing), instead of attempting to plan for the normal human inter-activity that takes place between diverse members of any group of people, any community – the more subjective social activity involving communication through human language. That is why naíonraí, gaelscoileanna, youth clubs and buildings and such – objective measures - are mentioned so often in these reports. It is not that these are not important, especially since they place institutions of cultural development back into the possession of the speech community, but that in themselves they are not sufficient. It is possible then to discern a certain disappointment in the authors that the aim they set themselves - an abstract aim, the revival of the Irish language – proved to be a lot more difficult and that the results of their labours appear limited. They see the weaknesses and list them in their articles. We hear an echo of this in Pilib Ó Ruanaí's question: cause or communication? Is the cause lost at times in communication, in the busy planning that helps to create the impression of an ambitious programme? Normally there are two reasons for a person to embrace a language: the cultural reason and the practical instrumental reason. It is important that both sources of motivation are satisfied.

Reflections

Certainly, it is important to start with aims and measurable targets and support systems to achieve the stated ends; that consultation occurs and co-operation that confers ownership of the plan on each participant agent at every level; that continuous monitoring is ensured and cohesion of all activities. But that is work based largely on paper and on talk, even if it also is based on research and on knowledge. It might even be described as technical work accomplished by technocrats. This is not to denigrate this stage of planning but rather to draw attention to the missing element. A language plan is not complete without clear realisation that its end is a social act; a social act resulting in linguistic behaviour by every member of the community to which the plan is directed if the plan is to be truly effective. The psychological aspects and the sociological aspects are as important as any other aspect in this planning. The contributors understood this intuitively, even if they have not managed to reach their destination – as yet.

Certain questions must be posed: what exactly is our desired aim; how do we define our community; what do we consider a fruitful result? Since language is a social act between people, a mere plan will not inspire a community. There appears to be a crucial relationship between language matters and the emotions. An effective message, occasion or event can awaken people. This effect cannot be ignored – but it is very seldom we see people's spirit mentioned in a plan. Yet these people as group are the effective target of the plan on paper.

On the other hand, some members of the community and language workers in particular must be committed to the cause in order to keep the flame of the required spirit alive. This is not sentimentality but a practical requirement of continuity. In the business sector it is called loyalty to the corporate mission statement. The contributor from Derry believes that fine buildings are not enough, but that an intellectual legacy must be engendered through them that will give strategic direction to the revival and to language planning. An act in the cause of a language community or in the cause of language in the community is similar to any charitable or philanthropic act: it is in the cause of common humanity that it is taken. Plans are all the poorer when this subjective element is omitted.

As in the case of classrooms of mixed ability or of mixed social background, it is important to empower everyone in the group to participate, a factor that is identified in the difficulties highlighted by the contributors. The importance of the community is recognised more today as an essential part of participative democracy. To this end, and on the grounds that the nature of community is continually changing, fragmenting, eroding, the Taoiseach established a group in 2005 to ensure that the best social traits are not lost to civil society. Likewise, in the European Union there has been much discussion on this subject towards the well-being of the citizen.

In language planning it is also crucial to differentiate between plans, policies and projects. A comprehensive policy that complements other plans and policies across all State concerns at every level – local, regional and national – is something currently rare in Ireland. Language projects or initiatives have a much more limited scope and focus in the context of the whole community; naíonraí or youth clubs fall into this category. Irish experience appears still to be based predominantly on individual unconnected initiatives, or schemes, or pilot projects – however worthy – rather than inclusive integrated language planning.

It is not easy to look into the future but it is on the future that any form of planning is directed. It would be a pity, however, not to learn from the past, from the examples that are available - from Bord na Gaeilge community schemes of twenty years past; from recent Conradh na Gaeilge schemes funded by Foras na Gaeilge; from the multifarious initiatives that have received funding from various programmes developed by Foras; from those supported by Údarás na Gaeltachta or from other small but valuable projects that have as yet received recognition only in their own communities; but especially from this publication.

There is a wonderful wealth of experience in these reports. They constitute an impressive first, not available elsewhere. They provide an excellent start for future planning based on analysis and comprehensive study of these individual cases. We are greatly indebted to the contributors for their clarity and openness and to the fortunate communities they represent.

The Authors

The Authors

Peadar Mac an Iomaire

Peadar is a former Chairperson of the Steering Committee of Glór na nGael. He is well known as a Gaeltacht community activist since the days of the Gaeltacht Civil Rights Campaign. He is the CEO of Acadamh na hOllscolaíochta Gaeilge, in the National University of Ireland Galway.

Lorcán Mac Gabhann

Above all else, Lorcán Mac Gabhann is a proud parent of four children, Clíona, Ciarán, Séadhna and Siún. He has been Ceannasaí (Head) of Glór na nGael since 2002. Before that he worked for Foras na Gaeilge and Conradh na Gaeilge. He regards his involvement in in the establishment of Gaelscoil Thaobh na Coille in south County Dublin in 1995 as a key achievement. The school now has more than 220 children being educated completely through Irish.

The Authors

Seán Mac an tSíthigh

Seán Mac an tSíthigh works with Comhchoiste Ghaeltacht Uíbh Ráthaigh in south Kerry as Heritage and Language Officer. He was awarded an M. Phil. from University College Cork in 2001 and has had a number of articles published on aspects of the folklore of Uíbh Ráthach and Corca Dhuibhne.

Caitlín Bhreathnach

Caitlín Bhreathnach began working with Comhchoiste Ghaeltacht Uíbh Ráthaigh in south Kerry in 1999 and was appointed Manager in 2003. She attended University College Cork where she was awarded a degree in Commerce in 1994 and she has since been awarded an MA with the IPA (Institute of Public Administration).

The Authors

Seosamh Mac Donncha

Seosamh Mac Donncha was raised with Irish in Baile an Doirín, County Galway. After post-primary education in Coláiste Éinde, he attended UCG (University College Galway) where he was awarded a First Class Honours in Celtic Studies. In December 2001 he was appointed CEO (Chief Executive Officer) of Foras na Gaeilge taking up the position on 1 February 2002. He recently took up the post of CEO with County Galway Vocational Education Committee. Married to Peig Ní Chéidigh from Leitir Móir, they have three children.

Bríde de Róiste

Bríde de Róiste has been working with the Irish language in Carlow for almost thirty years. She is the príomhoide (principal) of Gaelscoil Eoghan Uí Thuairisc and is very proud of the advances made by that school since it opened with twenty junior infants in 1982. The school has a current roll of 470.

The Authors

Eoghan Mac Cormaic

Eoghan Mac Cormaic was born in Derry in 1955. He was imprisoned and sentenced to life in 1976 and he learned Irish in the H Blocks. When he was released in 1991 he attended UCG (University College Galway) and was awarded a degree in Celtic Studies in 1995 and a Diploma in Community Development in 2003. He was Chairperson of the Sinn Féin Culture Department in the 1990s. He is married to Alison and lives in East Galway with their four children. Employed by Glór na nGael since 2005, he is currently Tánaiste of Conradh na Gaeilge.

Proinsias Ó hAilín

Proinsias Ó hAilín was born in Dublin in 1940. A secondary school teacher by profession, he taught for two years in Africa. After returning from Africa he was appointed teacher of Irish and English in Coláiste Pháirc Mhaoile, Clondalkin in 1966. He married Caitlín Ní Ríordáin in 1970 and they settled in Rathcoole. They have a family of five and it is a source of pride to Proinsias that he never spoke English to any of his children. He was appointed príomhoide (principal) in Coláiste Chilliain in 1981. At the turn of the century he retired after nineteen years as príomhoide. He has been Chairperson of Muintir Chrónáin for more than twenty years.

The Authors

Brian Mac Aongusa

Brian has spent most of his working life with the broadcast media. He played a prominent part in the campaign for Irish language television and was the first Chairperson of Comhairle Theilifís na Gaeilge (Council for Irish language television). He is also an author and has published several books.

Gearóid Ó hEára

Born in Derry, Gearóid has an honours degree in Irish Studies and a Diploma in Adult and Continuing Education. His interest in education is borne out by the role he has played in promoting gaeloideachas (Irish medium education) in Derry and his role on the Board of Governors of Gaelscoil Éadain Mhóir in Derry. Between 1983 and 1999 he was a member of the Sinn Féin Ard-Chomhairle. He is a member of Foras na Gaeilge and is CEO (Chief Executive Officer) of An Gaeláras in Derry, the largest centre for Irish and Irish language services in Ireland.

The Authors

Pilib Ó Ruanaí

Pilib Ó Ruanaí was born in the Short Strand in Belfast in 1959. He still lives there with his wife Sinéad, five daughters and one grandson. He learned Irish while on the Blanket protest in the H Blocks in the late 1970s. He was awarded a degree in Celtic and English in QUB and is presently studying for a Master's in Business Administration.

One of the founders of An Droichead, he is presently Chairperson of the organisation. He is the CEO (Chief Executive Officer) of Iontaobhas na Gaelscolaíochta (Funding Trust) in Belfast.

Seán Ó Dáimhín

Seán is a former political prisoner from Strabane. He learned Irish amongst his comrades in Crumlin Road and in Long Kesh. He was released from prison in December 1995 and has been working with the Irish language since then. He is a member of Craobh Mhic Chrosáin of Conradh na Gaeilge in Strabane and is Chair of the Board of Governors in Gaelscoil Uí Dhochartaigh. He is also a member of Gaelphobal, an umbrella group of Irish language bodies in Strabane, Gortin and Castlederg. He is Irish language officer of Sigersons GAA and for the past six years has been working as Irish Language Development Officer with Donegal County Council. He is married to Gina, and they have two daughters Grian (8) and Neasa (5) whom they are raising through Irish.

The Authors

Ariel Killick

From Sydney in Australia, Ariel Killick left her native shores to settle in Ireland in the year 2000. She began learning Irish in 1997 and has been working since then with language courses, the media, translation as an accredited translator and the arts. She is now living in Dublin.

Helen Ó Murchú

Helen is a former Chairperson of the Steering Committee of Glór na nGael.